Today,
SHE IS

Today, SHE IS

Molly Miltenberger Murray

RESOURCE *Publications* • Eugene, Oregon

TODAY, SHE IS

Copyright © 2013 Molly Miltenberger Murray. All rights reserved. Except for brief quotations in critical publications or reviews, no part of this book may be reproduced in any manner without prior written permission from the publisher. Write: Permissions. Wipf and Stock Publishers, 199 W. 8th Ave., Suite 3, Eugene, OR 97401.

Scripture taken from the New King James Version®. Copyright © 1982 by Thomas Nelson, Inc. Used by permission. All rights reserved.

Resource Publications
An Imprint of Wipf and Stock Publishers
199 W. 8th Ave., Suite 3
Eugene, OR 97401

www.wipfandstock.com

ISBN 13: 978-1-62564-461-9

Manufactured in the U.S.A.

This story is written for any, and for every,
reader that it helps.

There is plenty to say to everyone, but one thing really:
look both ways.

Contents

Acknowledgments / ix
Introduction / xi

PART I / 1

PART II / 9

PART III / 21

PART IV / 34

PART V / 46

PART VI / 67

PART VII / 80

Epilogue / 87
Bibliography / 89

Acknowledgments

THANKS TO MY FRIENDS who have given me so much of themselves.

Thanks especially to JanJan for sharing her story and her excitement for life.

So many thanks to my very dear friend from high school who wishes to remain anonymous; she kept a journal of my accident, and she has taught me how to be a faithful friend since we met 14 years ago.

Thank you to Aunt Eugenie for teaching my first-ever class in creative writing, for being such a wonderful if unwitting story-telling mentor, and for bringing me back to my roots with the coziest and most inspiring of homes for the three months that I wrote this.

Thank you Mary Claire Miltenberger for your help and encouragement footnoting and story-telling.

Thank you Gordon Murray for your help editing and footnoting, for supporting me and loving me through every day and a honeymoon book, and for making me happy.

Thanks fam for being the best and for not pulling the plug then or since.

Thanks be to God from Whom all blessings flow.

Introduction

THE SUMMER THAT I was 15, I was hit by a speedboat. I had a miraculous survival, and I had the next three tenuous, painful years to figure out how far I would recover. That was high school.

During those three years, I would have given anything to talk to someone who had undergone a similar recovery and who had come out the other side. Recovery from a freak accident is lonely enough; experiencing a head injury is intensely isolated. I was trapped inside my head: I empathized with those trapped inside of burning buildings, locked inside the Titanic, or otherwise caught in a cataclysmic and unavoidable turn of fate.

I related to the world through reading and I understood it through writing about it. Although no one that I actually knew seemed to go through any of the same issues, the treasury of literature that I read seemed to catch and express the turbulence and emotion of my experience. Even though I was too exhausted to engage in even the most inactive of activities, I could still pick up a book or listen to a recording, most of the time.

After I balanced enough that I could hide myself away, I intentionally blocked and burned as much as I could: but after college, I was still reeling from flashbacks and aftershock. I knew I had to tell my story to really let it go.

Introduction

My mom saved a stack of pictures from the flames: I began with these and embarked on a journey through old journals, old letters, old books, any part of myself that I had not literally burned. My old journals, found hidden in a cardboard box in the barn loft, recorded every step of my recovery. The book of quotes that I kept was even more insightful.

I unlocked my lost self by finding and experiencing these sources again. It was an extraordinarily successful and painful process to re-trace my steps and recreate the flashbacks: but as I understood what I went through, the fragments came together and I could finally reconcile with the past. I haven't had a flashback since.

I did not include many medical details in my endeavor to present an authentic experience. I ignored and avoided them as much I could during high school, and I still think they are distracting. I have yet to meet anyone who has had a speedboat land on their head, but I meet people every place I go that share the experience of mental trauma and the experience of pain.

I'll just give it away right here and now: the point of this book is to share my experience. This is the book that I wished I had in high school. It's for people who honestly want to understand some of the issues of recovery and that want to know what it feels like to recover from a life-impacting head injury. And now that it's down on paper, I can let it go.

> *"Then the Lord answered Job out of the whirlwind, and said: Now prepare yourself like a man; I will question you, and you shall answer Me."*[1]

---

1. Job 40:6–7.

PART I

Since yesterday, a century has passed away.
— Jean Lafitte[1]

THESE DAYS I AM waking up, and I am walking into a conscious dream where I am choked by the smell of a twisted forest that is the mint-green shade on the cover of those old Serendipity books about unicorns and trolls. It smells so densely of Bath & Bodyworks Bamboo Forest that I am seasick. I lunge and fall unconscious.

"Since yesterday a century has passed away," said Mssr. Jean Lafitte. I sentenced how the rough-battled captain had meant these words every day for a long long time of my life. In one day he had won a battle and his world had changed.

It takes only a day to overturn a world and to build a new one. A man in his prime has fought in the morning only to be plucked from the fray like a flower in the afternoon to be buried in the soil in the lightly falling rain of twilight while his sweetheart watched the setting sun from her porch and the breeze that carried away her heart left a void, she stood there twined around the porch column and

1. Eliot, *Middlemarch*, 382.

Today, SHE IS

did not know that the childrens' childrens' children of her and him together would not be playing a melody on the guitar in a hundred and twenty years.

Before Christian, the family stretches out for time immemorial in a French village in Alsace-Lorraine, attending court, mowing fields, paying the tributes of fashion and philosophy. Christian left the family chateau and escaped the guillotine by beginning anew, a plantation owner in the sugar fields of Haiti.

Waking up is such a miraculous event, every time. First there is the rushed confusion of a turbulent wood-between-the-worlds, half withdrawal of the land on the other side and part the scene that is in front of your open eyes, that is now taking over the world that before reigned in your mind.

It happens every arousal more or less quickly, more or less completely. There are so many worlds in the mind of a single person — every era, every mood, every day, sometimes, a world in itself to be entered or quitted. The less full is the awakening the stronger is the tangled bouquet-scent of a world that leaves a fragment in your mind so that you are never fully free from a day that became a world.

All that we call spirit and art and ecstasy only means that for one awful moment we remember that we forget: hats off to the great G.K.[2]

On the day the fires went up, Christian took his wife Marie Aimee's hand, and running out the back door, he escaped the violence of revolution for the second time. The ship with Christian and Marie Aimee on it came into the port of New Orleans. Stepping off the boat, they rolled into the city. They would make it like their home in France.

---

2. Chesterton, *Orthodoxy*, 72.

PART I

Waking up, walking outside of the door of your mind and standing on the porch for a bit, drinking it in, the brilliant sunlight streaming through the pines, sitting in the lap of the world. Mossy paths run through the yard like veins and you take the one that leads to a camellia bush the size of an armoire. Dew, dark glossy leaves, bright lipstick pink flowers in the fresh morning sun, the air crisp and warm wrapping you like a terry cloth towel. It is the most beautiful day in the world. This is the day that the Lord has made: you shall be glad and rejoice in it.

This is the day that is pasted in my mind as the standard for all other days to come, the picture of day in my first life. "Day" begins in the early morning in March on a porch in south Louisiana.

> *I shall not die, but live, and declare the works of the Lord. The Lord has chastened me severely, but He has not give me over to death.*[3]

The glare of white naked plastic pierces through the bluegray darkness and all that I know is that my body isn't here, but my mind is punctured by the smell of the white plasticity, of a very green and natural scent that is clean as acid. Like a ship the room heaves, up and then down every now and then; when I open my eyes to stare, it is askew like a room on a sailboat lodged sideways between rock and sea. From my shelf-bed underneath the white sheet the world is a dying yacht wrecked by the ungence of bamboo the white-green shade of a neon moth. It feels like the fifth watch of the night — sometime when the sun refuses to rise or to set in those nauseous, uncertain hours after the night and before the morning.

This is the first day of my second life.

---

3. Ps. 118:17.

Today, SHE IS

Christian was succeeded by Alphonse. Alphonse built the houses that are famous in the French Quarter for the curling Spanish iron for his wife. And the family lived in them past money, past TB and war.

The white house on the corner is the one where James and then Henry were born.

A very dear friend recorded a journal of the proceedings.

> *Aug. 4, 2002*
>
> *Dear Molly,*
> *We came to see you today. You did come out of the coma, so you're able to move and open your eyes, but most of the time you look around like a deer in the headlights. I talked to your folks who were glad you could move, but wished you were up and going again. It is so hard to be patient. Your eyes were slightly opened when I came into your room, you looked the same as before, but they had strapped your ankles and wrist so you wouldn't move so much. Your dad asked if you loved him, and if so squeeze his hand, and you squeezed a whole bunch! I hope they can take those pipes out of your throat soon, they must really hurt. I'll talk to you soon.*[4]

Everything is illusory, everything less vivid than a dream. All faces are blurred bobble heads to my unspectacled eyes, all distances deceptive, shallow as sand in clear water. Every object is a doorknob that my right hand is too weak to turn. Nurses are shadows talking at me. The world is alive when I close my eyes and become part of the night, watching the white room from odd corners, participating

---

4. Anon., *Journal*, Aug. 04, 2002.

PART I

through nostalgic dreams; until I open my eyes and the room is flooded with sunshine.

A fire-breathing dragon crawls up and retches itself from my throat. This is more like a flame swallower, a sword-swallower dragging a serrated edge up the sides of his throat and messing up the trick. I open my mouth until I swallow my face, and the hose rattles up my throat like a Model-T on a washboard road. I remember taking out the ventilator and learning how to breathe — in, out, in, out — *hah*, *hah*, *hah*, *hah*, not air enough to fog a mirror from my shredded throat.

And then I can see again. The world rushes towards me all at once as Mamma slides my glasses onto my face and the scene is framed in focus. Richie is unshaved-scruffy and man-tall; he is grown up. Mom and Dad are older. They are all grown up. After a while, it hits me that I must have somehow grown-up in the meantime too. I am alive and now I see.

But a boy that I think I know is putting my shoes on and I don't know how to keep both feet on the ground. Who is this man? Mom hands me onto a walker and we stumble through long hallways, one foot safely on the ground in front of the other with hands on either side.

I watch the building tops and the streetlights and the blue sky flicker past the windows from the ambulance bed all the way to the Rehab Center. You won't remember this, they said, you won't remember the I.C.U. No one ever does.

I do. I remember learning how to walk, and I remember the cock-eyed shots of buildings and sky-line through the window of the ambulance that brought me to the rehab center.

Now is surrounded by tubes and roses, white walls, Hallmark cards. The triangularity of the room wedges its way into the burgeoning reality of the world; the diagonal

Today, SHE IS

bed inserted into the corner becomes a mountain peak to be clung to.

"This is what happened." And again, "This is what happened." Over and over and over again, they say the same thing so many times, every time I open my eyes.

Someone is constantly reminding me that I have an arm on my left side. I meet lists of happy happy doctors and nurses who flip pictures, show me numbers, letters, ask me questions about the president, who is not Clinton any more, that's right, and practice walking.

Apricot juice is icy, orchard-fresh, sugar-sweet, sitting in a plastic mustard-yellow chair in a blanket. I don't eat the jello because the tray is such a nasty old-lady mustard-afghan color, the kind of plastic that you click your nails on. Aunt Eugenie tells me to eat it, because they can't make the food *that* bad. But they can try, I whisper in my hoarse voice that slips out so soft that soundwaves are unreal and immaterial. She thinks that is so funny. I didn't mean it as a joke.

Father, mother, sisters, brothers, aunts, uncles, cousins, others. An odd array of relatives and friends, acquaintances and strangers are here, sometimes some, sometime others, and the abnormality fits the disjunction of my now-life. Between them all everyone seems to be having lots of fun. They have so many funny stories to tell me that I have vague regrets that I am not a part of it.

I am bone-tired out by walking down the hallways holding on to a strong arm, or we sit in the wedge-room. Atrophied, they say about my broken knee.

The second or third day my blue baseball cap slips. There is a mirror, and I am wearing my glasses so I can look into it and see that most of my head is bald. Oh, so this is what they said. I should be dead, but I am alive. I am a miracle. The hair will come back.

PART I

My voice is shallowest of all, a ghost that tells me I can speak until I open my mouth and gape at air that is empty and dry as a desert. Words became real only because it hurts to talk and I push them out of an aching throat as if from a cheese grater. The little birds told me, humankind cannot bear very much reality.[5]

Old people who can barely hobble are here in the rehab center; young people are in the rehab center in baseball caps. Some people don't talk and some people can't think. A good amount of them won't ever rehabilitate enough to go home; some of them are rehabilitated enough to begin work pushing carts at Albertson's Groceries.

My mind is a vault with a few corners of things I have heard in the rehab hospital, the darkness haunted with the harpies of weird dreams. I learned how to count straight yesterday; today before we left they explained how to find names in a phone book. I am one, two, three, four, five, six days out of a coma — maybe seven, depending on how you count it. They say it will come back. It will all come back.

Oh give thanks to the Lord for He is good! For His mercy endures forever.[6]

Take Cathy, Mike, the bearded male nurse, is saying. Now Cathy's a heart-warming case. Smart girl, smart as a whip, top of her class in law school, engaged to a handsome young guy. Everyone thought she would die — got in a car wreck just before Christmas — but nope! No, no, that was a happy story. We thought she'd be a vegetable. But I tell you, that girl walked out of the rehab center herself after three months, and is as happy and as sweet as can be. She's good friends with her old fiancé and his wife, and is supporting herself. "I still see her from time to time," finishes bearded

---

5. Eliot, "The Four Quartets 1: Burnt Norton."
6. Ps. 118:1.

Today, SHE IS

Mike in his chlorine green scrubs fondly, "When she bags my groceries at Albertson's she loves to say hi."

"Poor girl," I mouthe, trying not to cry. Mike is the first person I have met who I do not like, no, not at all, and I don't know why. The vibe attaches to me like a burr in my sock.

"Why?" he asked; "She is happy, her family is happy; she was a miracle. Customers love her. Take it from me, Cathy is one of the lucky ones." He said that I wouldn't remember him.

Lewis Thomas wrote that notions become as sea-creatures, decorated all over with other creatures living as symbionts.[7] Here in the white walls bleached free, there are no weeds.

I am fifteen. They say. I am a miracle. My one clue that all of this must be real is that here I am — and what seems normal to me is an aberration to everyone else. Here I am: alive, newly-birthed, my mind swept free of the past like a whiteboard.

I think that you have never seen a morning washed so clean.

---

7. Thomas, *The Lives of a Cell*, 143.

PART II

For ask now concerning the days that are past, which were before you, since the day that God created man on earth, and ask from one end of heaven to the other, whether any great thing like this has happened, or anything like has been heard.[1]

MY OWN FACE KEEPS flashing into my mind, a picture of my own tanned face with bobbed blonde above my lavender tankini. Wheat-tanned hills lope behind it and the spray spatters onto it, almost, but the lakedrops slither down the memory squarely, as though it's a picture with a glass window-pane in front of the face.

Let me take you through the hall. The room is monumental: the ceilings are twice the height they are in normal house, and the crown molding holds it in like the ribbon on a dress of Marie Antoinette. The heavy furniture, an armoire, daybeds, a couch, is heavy black wood twisted like a grapevine and polished like a candlestick. The room is upholstered a long time ago. Little curios — ivory boxes, statuettes, South Pacific shells — line the tables and nook in

1. Deut. 4:32.

Today, SHE IS

drawers. What you notice when you are racing through the room in the shadows at night, past the side of the table that goes on forever that used to be the door of an abbey, are the people on the wall.

A mallet comes down squarely on the frame and the glass is shattered, fragmented on the wooden slats of the dock. Pieces of the broken face flutter to the ground, shreds of magazine print dripping in a pool of blood.

Souvenirs of present personality are terrifying when the subjects are so long dust and wreaths of hair framed in gilt. Their dust is shelved in the marble family mausoleum in the St. Louis Cemetery of New Orleans. Their stories shape the air around them like the frame of a house.

The great green porch creaks like the house is moving. These wooden floors are never without footsteps. Heritage drapes on our family like the spring blue mist in the morning in south Louisiana, barely there and almost too bright to see through, laying on your shoulders like mosquito netting and glistening at your feet.

My grandmother, Barbara, was 15 when her mother died, succumbed to consumption. She was with her in the apartment in Houston, all alone when her mother took her last breath. The neighbors took her in for the few days before her father came back from traveling.

I was 15 when I thought I died, surrounded by family. They never knew I'd live.

They prayed that I would.

You can always tell a good artist by the eyes. They should follow you wherever you appear from — the side of the room, the door, the corner. These portraits are masterpieces. They are so real that I have almost caught them out of the frames so many times, nearly, almost there. They are

PART II

life-size: larger than life, seeping life from the oil as I race past them, sent to bed.

The moss on the rock face of the Holter Canyon clutches to the niches in between eagles nests and ancient bristled bonsai-like pine trees, the only bryophyta of its kind found in the world. The water in the river snaking in the narrow channel beneath is glacier fresh and so blue, so dark mallard blue, icy and 3,000 feet deep, someone said.

Lewis and Clark, the explorers, came through this place on the Missouri on their journey to the Pacific Coast. Legend has it that, ensconced in the channel, they watched the cliffs swing shut in a silent rocky clasp and said, "Let us call this the Gates of the Mountains."

The men in our family have many things in common—a nose, a laugh, but one is distinct and I remember family friends remarking on it: their wives are dearly beloved. Christian had two. When Amelie died, he repainted her white dress black and the portrait remained in the living room, to her chagrin. She has a portrait too, with her twin sons. The one on the right riding the tricycle died while the portrait was being painted. He is larger in the picture than he would have been in real life. The one on the left is the one that lived. Henry is the son of Edwin, the son of James, the son of Alphonse, the son of Christian.

Most of them died not long after the pictures were painted. The Munster Boy did not live past age 12. The second twin on the tricycle died long before the portrait was ever painted. I don't even know the name of the Munster girl. Aristide the Judge grew old and left a will. Amelie, beloved wife, was in white when the likeness was taken. Her dress was painted over in black after she and the child died in childbirth. They are all dark-haired, dark-eyed, sweet-mouthed, Roman-nosed.

Today, SHE IS

Amelie, the first wife, is the most remarkably like-life. The others can die of boredom, possibly, but she is a question that crawls up your spine and keeps her creepily alive in the conversation of the room. As people have said on the subject of Mona Lisa, there is much to be said for a lady who preserves her mystery for 200 years.

Does that even happen? Does a driver ever really just, turn without looking, like that, speeding towards you, not thinking, not turning, not turning, not turning, straight on forward until he ramps up the side of your pontoon boat and lands on your daughters?

The speedboat with the upturned snub nose leaves a snotty crest in the river. The driver doesn't take the trouble to check for a clear coast before he shoves up the boat's nose and turns, and doesn't take the trouble after. He's on a pleasure-ride.

A pontoon boat is a family-sized craft, an oversized raft made for floating and leisurely chugging. It cannot move fast. It certainly cannot race out of the path of a speedboat.

Our pontoon boat is a sitting duck of screaming people while the speeding speedboat speeds onward and does not hear the screams of disbelief, the final, desperate belief.

Little daguerrotypes are on the tables with lockets and miniatures. A wreath of cousin someone's hair is on the wall, with smaller wreaths of locks and a painted Chinese screen, ivory encases the table-top. The larger wreathe belongs to the Bride.

My cousins look strikingly like them.

The most poignant image, I think, is this, the dark oil seeping out of the engine and churning in the water like blood. It happens.

PART II

An Anglo-Saxon poem I read my sophomore year in high school had a line that licks round your tongue. Wyrd goes ever as it must.[2]

> *"Is he going to hit us?" screamed a younger sister, while my aunt shrieked, "Do something!" In an exceptionally slow pontoon, it was too late to do anything and we had to sit terrified in the peace and loveliness of Holter Lake for the speedboat to come crashing into our bow, landing over my two youngest sisters and on top of me.*[3]

My brother is ready to leap gallantly into the cold dark river to search for us. Dad tells the police report that he and my uncle had pushed off the boat, but they had not; Daddy pushed the boat that covered my two youngest sisters and me back into the water.

Barbara Ellis, aged 4 years old, brown curly hair and round cheeks, knocking on the door of the tall white shotgun mansion next door, New Orleans. "Miz Miltenberger! Miz Miltenberger! Can I play with Henry?" Henry Miltenberger, 5 years old, freckly, red-haired, lanky already, lopes to the front porch, overjoyed. Mrs. Miltenberger disappears into the dark hall and Barbara throws rocks at Henry. That'll teach him. Teach him who's smart!

> *My father and uncle shoved the assassin-boat into the river, freeing my sisters, who were for the most part unharmed, and myself, who looked — dead. From my bench on the boat I was sped by helicopter to the nearest hospital in Great Falls, Montana where for the first week doctors and nurses scur-*

---

2. Heaney, *Beowulf*, l. 455.
3. "A Severe Mercy," the account of the experience that I wrote after rehab.

> *ried around to save me as I lay unconscious in a coma in my room in the Intensive Care Unit.*[4]

In the picture my sister told me one night I am unconscious, with a single line of blood trickling down from my forehead from where I was scraped by the rough. The little girls are awake and crying — everyone is crying. I throw up, and I start breathing again. The pontoon slowly chugs across the lake, all the way back to the landing, and I am flown to Great Falls by the emergency helicopter on the dock.

Henry stepped out of school at age 15. His favorite teacher had taken him aside. Henry, he said, you aren't doing us any good, and we certainly aren't doing you any good. When his father took him along on an interview for his brother Gus. The job was offered to Henry. Henry went to work at the ports at age 15.

> *Dear Molly,*
> *When Mom and I arrived around 4:00 p.m., we weren't allowed to see you. You were on a sedative drip to calm you and to stop your thrashing. Every hour they would stop the sedative, causing the pain to hit you immediately to check where you were. One time they asked you to open your eyes and they thought they saw you open them a touch. Another time a nurse was changing your I.V. when you sat up and opened your eyes from the pain. The nurse said your eyes were glazed and couldn't see.*
>
> *We prayed for you in the chapel, and I am spreading the news so the whole nation will be praying for you. I wish I could have seen you, there are times I don't believe it has happened, and other times I can't stop crying. I have been*

---

4. "A Severe Mercy."

PART II

> *praying for a miracle, that you will once again be healed and new. . . I wish with all my heart that you were healthy at home and I could call to talk your ear off!*
> *Love,*
> *Your Friend*[5]

Since three days ago a lifetime is past. Since yesterday a century has passed away. The whole world prays for me; at least this country prays, and some churches in Europe. There is no brain activity at all.

Barbara was 16 when she joined her brother Sydney at Tulane. The youngest in her class.

The injury is more serious than they thought. I'm not waking up like I should, and I'm shivering, sweating, there's a fever in my brain. My traumatized brain is encaged by a coma from a severe shock to my occipital glob, swelling to a balloon inside of my fractured skull. Soon it is going to pop.

The doctors consider my blank brain a lost case by Wednesday. My mind is irrecoverable, and my life is scarcely closer.

They give me up for lost. My parents don't. They are always with me, praying for me, talking to me, playing music. Daddy rubs my feet and the nurses cry because fathers don't usually care this much. Mummy paints my nails and the nurses call me Sleeping Beauty.

Four days and the medical team says to pull the plug.

Our family line has a very distinct nose. Aquiline in some. Roman in most. Roman, I'll say Roman, a friend told my dad, it's roamin' all over your face. My great-grandfather told my grandfather that what he left to him was not money but a good name. Our family does not always have brains. We don't always have beauty. But the one trait we

---

5. Anon., *Journal*, July 2002.

Today, SHE IS

can all account for is character. I come from a family of personalities.

Dr. Gorsuch is a man my parents trust. He's the best in the unit, a Christian, and he is willing to take a risk. He suggests a procedure that gives me a 50/50—40/60—30/70—20/80—10/90, 5/95, 1/100? A chance of survival; prospects unknown.

I am one of the first. There isn't a precedent, but there isn't a choice.

Henry and Barbara are my grandparents.

My parents, distraught. Praying in the chapel; giving me back to God. There is a verse that they hold onto for dear life, Psalm 118:17. *I shall not die, but live, and declare the works of the Lord. The Lord has chastened me severely, but He has not given me over to death.*[6]

> *Dear Molly,*
> *Your brain was expanding so much they thought they might have to do surgery, and you had a fever to make things worse. But today, they cooled your temperature to around 95°F, and put you on a paralyzing drug so you wouldn't shiver, causing your brain to get worse. So far the swelling has gone down a bit and we're all thanking the Lord. Since they put you in a kind of coma, they won't be taking you out of it until they are positive you are better, you won't be able to move for a little while. I'm still having a hard time believing that you're in the hospital fighting for your life. I was given a picture blown up from my birthday of your family and me, every time I look at your beautiful face I can't believe something awful could happen to our darling Molly. You are such a blessing to know and I can't wait to see you alive and well. I love*

---

6. Ps. 118:17.

PART II

you. God, please heal Molly and help her family to be comforted.[7]

Daddy says that his father never, never talked about the war. There is a bronze medal in a box with his uniform, a compass, a knife. Poppy mentioned once that he had been attacked with the knife in face to face combat, and now he is holding the knife that was held to his face.

They swathe me in ice like a dead fish, which reduces the swelling in my brain, and keeps it within reasonable limits. I am always cold.

He ran out of his shelter into the snow of German fields once in his socks, almost dragging his best friend—wait, I'm putting on my boots—before he could put the boots on, the camp was blown apart, Henry watching.

And I live.

Aug. 31, 2002

Dear Molly,
I am so excited that I was able to see you today! I was able to sneak in under the nurse's nose and see you. You look so peaceful. I could only see your nose up and your hands. You have so many tubes coming out of you, to help you breathe, suck out your stomach acid so you don't vomit from hunger and just a whole bunch of tubes that I don't know what they do. The doctors shaved a square on your head to put a brain pressure antenna thing on your head to read your brain's pressure. The nurse put your hair in pigtails, you look cute. When we prayed your dad said I could hold your hand, it was so soft and cold, your hands are always so pretty and soft. Your brain pressure is at 10-18 but it jumped up to 20 and dropped to 2

---

7. Anon, *Journal*, July 2002.

Today, SHE IS

> *(when they were sucking the phlegm out of your lungs so you wouldn't get pneumonia). Normal is -2 to 2. Your parents stroke you and play soft music to make the pressure go down. The doctor gave you an EEG test to see if your brain works or not, and it came out positive! Get well my dearest Molly.*
>
> *God hears us, trust Him.*[8]

Mere was a WAC, one of the info girls in the army who wore those adorable olive shifts and sifted through important information and decoded messages. At a ball in D.C., she danced with distinguished generals and charmed a European prince.

These days I am waking up on a kitchen counter, and I close my eyes so they won't know that I am awake because I don't want to talk. The room closes around me like a curtain, like I am a child squinting out from under the covers, trying not to be seen by the babysitter. People move through the shadowed whiteness of the plastic-smoothened room. Here I am, peering out from under the blankets at them, and they don't even know it. Bright white people dressed in white dress-suits, the kind from Dillard's that old ladies wear with gold jewelry, stop whispering in the background and move closer, so close that I know they'll pinch my shoulder like an old man, and then so close again that I realize I've closed my eyes — so I open them again and up goes the room.

After the war, Mere went back to Tulane to get her masters in biochemistry. When she ducked out of the program to get married, her professor railed at her — you'll have eight children and you'll deserve it for leaving! Guess I will! Said Barbara. And she left to marry Henry, and had eight children. My father is the youngest.

8. Anon., *Journal*, July 31, 2002.

PART II

August 2, 2002

Dear Molly,
Today, your brain pressure is sticking around 10, which is good! You have an ever so slight fever, but not a bad one. I heard you opened your eyes and looked around today, but they couldn't tell if you could see or not. You are able to move and crossed your feet and such. They hope to take you off the sedative slowly and have you wake up! Love ya.[9]

I remember floating at the level of Daddy's head at the wake, seeing my grandfather in a box. It was the first time I had ever seen Daddy cry; I could not bear it. People think there is no way that I could remember Poppy; he died when I was one and a half. But he called me Molly Ellen. I remember him catching me with his feet, tickling me from his Laz-Y-Boy by the door, teasing us cousins on the front porch, and how he looked in his box at the funeral.

Some people remember every moment of being in a coma, not being able to speak, the trap, the muzzle of silence. One gentleman lived for 23 years trapped within himself, clinically dead, until a physician worked with him and he communicated that he was alive beneath it all, trapped, trapped. He cannot get out. He cannot get out — 23 years. Now he is writing a book by signaling.

What is it like? Not horrific. It is a string of real-to-life, realer-than-life, dreams, bringing me back to places that I haven't been to in years. I am ten years old and find a dumpster with a bear in it in Grand Lake, Colorado. I am four years old and cross a bridge over the monkey house of the Brookfield Zoo in Chicago.

Passing through hallways and tunnels of darkness and light, falling down a hole of life like Alice in Wonderland.

9. Anon., *Journal*, Aug. 2, 2002.

Today, SHE IS

Mere's funeral was in the spring in the Abbey, which always reminds me of Easter. At the wake, my sister younger fought my third cousin because she said her shoes were prettier. My cousins and I played cards behind the curtains until we were too noisy and attracted an aunt, and I cried at the graveside.

At Aunt Dolly's funeral — that woman was a saint — her daughters asked us to kiss her cheek. A band broke out into *When All the Saints Come Marching In* when the pallbearers carried her up the aisle, and we all sang along and ate cake with blue frosting.

I almost died too. But — I lived. I was 4, but now I am 15, again, oddly enough, and starting over, against the odds. Despite the odds. The hospital calls me the miracle girl. I am a miracle.

All the time — every five, ten waking minutes, they tell me the story again and again. I shall not die but live: and declare the works of the Lord. The Lord has chastened me severely, but He has not given me over to death. I was crushed by a flying boat and here I am. Life is a paradox that doesn't fit in my hatbox, and death is only the beginning of it.

An ancient Asian proverb tells that we cannot talk about life until we have eaten bread salted with a tear.

PART III

AFTER WALKING HIS YOUNGEST daughter down the aisle in January of 1991, William Brock stopped in the middle of a sentence. He put his hand to his head — "Oh my," he said, sitting in his den, and falling unconscious, into a coma, undergoing a ruptured cerebellar artery aneurism.

He didn't breathe. He didn't breath, says JanJan, shaking her head; and I knew that he had oxygen for he had a pulse. And just about the time I was ready to start the CPR, he began to inhale with the most ethereal sound — I have never heard a sound like it in my entire life. He just kept breathing in, and in, and in, inhaling, with this mysterious sound, it was like he filled from his neck to his hips, And I thought — 'he's going to explode' — and then, there was a little pause, and he began to exhale, with an equally mysterious sound, but totally different. Black and white different. I can't explain it. He did that three times, only, before the ambulance got there. I just think that God breathed into him — I really do.[1]

The Voice told the man to lie down and he did, stretching himself across the exuberant green grass and letting his muscles melt into the earth as he closed himself and fell

---

1. Janelle Brock, interview with author, Moscow, Idaho, September 2010.

Today, SHE IS

asleep. Some time later the man opened his eyes and saw her — there she was, doe-eyed, hair trussed, elongated by his side. And time passed by like the revolutions of triumphant stars as they stared into each other's eyes: first man and first woman, he made of earth and she made of him, and the furry things pattering round.

The stories that I had grown up reenacting in felt figure pictography in Sunday School were strange tales less akin to me than The Battle of Gilead. I was conscientiously born again to Jesus when I was one and a half years old, cross my heart: my mind was cleaned like a slate when I was 15. Now the Bible unfolds epic, passionate master tale of history, novel, mystery, and creative non-fiction.

Where ever I go I see burning bushes, objects on fire; when I look closely, I learn my own story, a story shadowed forth by the all-wise God. That's a paraphrase of Suzanne Clark in *Sketches of Home*.[2]

The sketch of my home is in Technicolor: it's completely a work of magic, a burning bush that I took for granted before.

My life is a miracle, a wonder—the more so because I am only alive enough to realize the miracle of every life. They didn't live. Those didn't recover. I lived and I am recovering: I did not die but lived to declare the works of the Lord.[3]

Take it and read, take it and read. That's what the little boy told St. Augustine in the garden.[4] You know the old Augustinian view of the world — it is a book, God's first book, hand-written and signed in a cryptic long-hand like a Bible we have to catch in motion.

---

2. Clark, *Sketches of Home*, 12.
3. Ps. 118:17.
4. Augustine, *Confessions*, IX:XII.

PART III

The local hospital told me that he might live a couple of hours. His brain was so filled with blood that all you could see was the outline of the skull.[5]

Inebriate of Air — am I — And Debauchee of Dew — Reeling — thro endless summer days — From inns of Molten Blue — Emily Dickinson.[6]

Life is la vie en rose. I am alive. I am loved. I love everyone in the whole world and the whole world is sparkling like pink champagne. I lived, and I am miraculously almost back to normal.

Give me till this summer. I am drinking life to the lees and boy, it tastes good. A ta sainte, mon cher! A ma sainte. To my sanity.

> *Dearest Molsy,*
>
> *I came over to your house today to play games and stuff. We played Yahtzee, and Stratego. You beat me on Yahtzee! You look like normal and you wear your hair in the cutest way folding your hair over your shaved spot and clipping it. It was so nice to be back at your place and kind of have a normal visit. I am so glad you're okay, you really did scare me.*
> *Love ya lots.*[7]

About the 10th day he went into total renal failure — total. It wasn't so much verses that kept me going, as hymns. I couldn't pray, but I could sing. I lived on songs, on old, old, old hymns.[8]

---

5. Brock, interview.
6. Dickinson, "I Taste a Liquor Never Brewed."
7. Anon., *Journal*, Sept. 2002.
8. Brock, interview.

Today, SHE IS

I am always, always, always floating skyward like a helium balloon because I am alive. I am the girl who lived. *Life is settling back to normal and life is better than before* my diary says, *I'm shaken out of my 'bourgeois-ness into a wonderful fairy-tale sort of exhilaration*.[9] I am Cinderella and Sleeping Beauty. That was what they called me in the hospital.

The great G.K. says that fairytales make rivers run with wine only to make us remember, for one wild moment, that they run with water.[10] My life is stayed in this ecstatic moment — but that is the worst word for it. Stayed? Echoing, ricocheting, from one moment of this euphoria to the next.

It has been a month and I feel that I am at least 80% recovered. Three years? Pish! I'll be fully recovered in 6 months, no doubt. I am just so tired — all I can do is rest, and then I rest from resting. But I will not begin by allowing this accident to interfere with normal life or I will never get back to normal life.

Then the doctor approached me and said there was no choice but to pull the plug. I didn't want to. It didn't feel right. And out of the corner of my eye, I saw Curtis, shaking his head No. He agreed with me that this was not the right decision. We needed to give him a few more days. And so that's what I told the doctor. Later, I thanked Curtis — and he said, that wasn't me. I wasn't there.[11]

Ten days after I come home I climb the stone steps to the great classical brick hall of Carroll College, where I join the intermediate French class at Carroll College that I have been planning to take all along before the accident. My tongue is stuck in the middle of my impeccable accent

---

9. My journal.
10. Chesterton, *Orthodoxy*, 72.
11. Brock, interview.

PART III

and *je ne trouve pas les mots pour les* most common things — but here I am, taking a college course. Three years? Pish!

> *Today it has been a month since I came home. I am so, so, SO tired I just want to fall into somebody's arms and cry. But I won't, because they said that might be one of the after-effects. I want to do French homework and write a newspaper article and practice piano and go upstairs to be with Aunt Margot and little Margot and Critter but I am just too tired. I am too tired to do anything but try to take a nap, or this. I've felt faint, and when I feel faint, I never remember what I say; it's a little scary. Perhaps I'm so tired from my reserve and continual constraint to be proper and only talk well — that would explain why I only want to babble on. I'm too tired to write more.*[12]

Bill, I don't know if you can hear me right now, I have no idea if you can hear me, but I'm going to describe this to you.

Finally, I convinced the doctor that he could understand me. It gave us hope to keep going.[13]

"Aren't I making your head ache?" said Harriet; "Damnably, but I like it," replied Lord Peter.[14] Dorothy Sayers is a good friend right now. Sometimes I am too tired to read, but nevertheless I devour Lord Peter. He is not handsome, but he is so attractive because he is a tragi-comic genius who is wrecked by bouts of amnesia and mental relapse.

I read every word of Sayer's biography, but all that I remember is that she had a child out of wedlock with a complete rift, and she describes the event of a childhood epiphany as the "magnificent moment when the intersecting

12. My journal.
13. Brock, interview.
14. Sayers, *A Cloud of Witnesses*, 163

circles marched out of the Euclid book and met on the green grass in the sun-flecked shadow of the mulberry tree."[15]

"But I was telling you about the standing frame," Jan-Jan catches her thoughts and begins again. He was strapped into the standing frame to build the leg muscles. He would stand up in the standing frame for thirty minutes at a time, strapped in it for thirty minutes at a time. That just seemed such a long time. The first time or two, I just sat, and watched. And then I thought, oh! Let's make this a little more fun. So I got a cassette player, and played 50s music and—we liked to dance, we jitterbugged a lot — so I put the jitterbug music on and hold his hand, and I danced in front of him, and it sort of felt like we were, kind of, dancing, and it made the time go by kind of faster.[16]

It is funny how much of your life revolves around memories. Constantly, my siblings talk about how we talked when we were little, about how we took Jack to the beach two years ago, about canoeing in the lake last summer, about the time we went to that restaurant when you were in the hospital.

I know it's expected that a brain injury leaves a victim without a personality or a past, but it makes me feel vaguely undressed, like I've mismatched my socks or forgotten a camisole or heaven forbid — my knickers. Remember that time when we did this all together and had the best time ever, ever, ever?

No, I don't.

I don't have memories.

We spent either 10 ½ or 11 months in the rehab facility, and I just watched him transform.[17]

15. Brabazon, *Dorothy Sayers: A Biography*, 26.
16. Brock, interview.
17. Brock, interview.

PART III

I've always thought that if you really wanted to remember What Would Jesus Do then a rainbow bracelet is probably not the way. It isn't. I know it now sure thing.

I'm wearing all of her old clothes and a sign around my neck that says What Would Molly Do? I still have no idea. Where is she? And what would she do? I am a stranger in a foreign body.

This is all to say that life comes to me as a shock, an electric eel darting out of a sea cave to light the benthic depths, for a moment. A slow current moving up my system that eventually reached my mind and I jolted alive to the fact, after three months of being home from the rehab hospital, that it might be just as the doctors say.

> *The doctors said that this would happen, that I would do something and think it was stupid a month later. Usually I am optimistic and bright; this has made me* [here I skip a couple of pages and, "oops, see?" my frustrated hand writes on the empty page] *despondent. I changed my paper that I had thought was ready last night—what is it* really *like? It makes my innards groan to think of that and my insides cry out with pain all over to wonder what else I have done without seeing. It must have hurt so much Mamma and Dad to see me so unperceiving.*[18]

I write in my journal. I want my words to be impeccable. Because although I fling between talking and talking and talking and caverns of introversion, I don't feel that I can ever communicate a thought outside of my head.

This is growing up again, again, all over again. A social faux pas that slips past when you are three, five, ten years old makes more of a splash at 15. At least to yourself.

---

18. My journal.

Today, SHE IS

Ben Folds says that Everybody knows it SUCKS to grow up.[19]

Bill, I don't know if you can hear me right now, I have no idea if you can hear me, but I'm going to describe this to you — and, finally, I convinced the doctor that he could understand me.

Oh, I saw him suffer, terribly. And they told me that he would not remember it — but I do. I remember all of it. It was torture.[20]

It suddenly dawns on me. I'm on page one. I have to re-learn everything. Not just something, everything. It is just that some things come fast. I can walk, read, balance, and multi-task, somewhat, acceptably fine by now. Social skills, every doctor chimes, are the last to come back.

These horrible thoughts hover outside my other ones so that I can see their shadows.[21]

When he was learning to speak — he could not speak a word — the therapist taught him where to put his tongue to make different sounds. To this day he still exercises his tongue, by putting it on every tooth, starting at the back, on one side, he puts it on every tooth and then moves back the other way. We don't think about where we place our tongue to make different sounds, but when you can't talk at all then you have to think about it — it's very complicated, very complicated.[22]

It does worry me though, just slightly. I don't remember what I was like. I don't want to act out of character; but

---

19. Folds, "Still Fighting It."
20. Brock, interview.
21. My journal.
22. Brock, interview.

PART III

I — don't have a character. There isn't a personality to direct my decisions.

Just look at de world around you, what more are you lookin' for?[23]

He would learn to say a word, and then he would perseverate — he would say that word over and over, not hundreds, but thousands of times. He would say it in a high pitch, in a low pitch, say it fast, and say it slow, he would slur it up, and down and — it was very irritating to me. One day we were in a hallway — I pushed him for miles and miles in the wheelchair. I just was tired of hearing him saying the same word. So I kneeled down by him and I said, "Bill, are you saying that same word just to practice, just to hear yourself — or can you just not help it?[24]

> *November 8, 2002*
>
> *I'm sleepy today. It's like I had been bitten by a tse-tse fly and had that disease that dad's friend got on a safari.*[25]

My eyes were twice their size when I looked up. I hated how easily I cried: emoticons of emotion were pinned to my sleeve. I was facing the world. I was facing the moment, the moment that had already passed in a flash of the future. To be the embarrassing one in the corner who missed the point, who couldn't color in the lines. You might not miss the chair when you sit down but be prepared, because you will very probably fall off of it with a loud crash anyway; you'll hurt your ankle and not tell.

When I am making a call I like to go to my room and use my pink phone. Then no one can see how long it takes

23. Menken/Ashman, "Under the Sea."
24. Brock, interview.
25. My journal.

Today, SHE IS

me to find a number in the phone book or to hit the right numbers on the keypad.

Life has a lot of sparkle and zest and smoothness after all. Of course.[26]

I am playing the piano. That is my best therapy. I begin it right away after I get home.

My left hand is so much slower than my right, and my right hand isn't quite connected to my mind. I feel every signal that is being sent — eye to the page to make the connection with the right note, which flies to my brain, to my fingers, both, ideally, at the same time. I am trying. I am trying hard.

And he had not spoken at all up to that point other than a word, and he just looked up at me, and, crystal clear, said: can't help it.[27]

I just read an article about assisted suicide. Before I didn't have an opinion besides "it's bad." Now I feel strongly — it literally made me sick.[28]

And I hear the thunder and like the great G.K. I see a power steam engine of long words rattling past us, carrying thousands, a horde, of those who are too tired or too indolent to walk or think or feel for themselves.[29]

So many people love me. I am so overwhelmed by it I want to cry. They love me so much they brought me back. My family loves me so much it is heartbreaking. My friends love me so much it is heart-breaking.

Part of therapy is to socialize, with the other patients, and it was really neat, touching, to see — how the patients help each other. Bill would meet to play checkers with this

26. My journal.
27. Brock, interview.
28. My journal.
29. Chesterton, *Orthodoxy*, 121.

PART III

young man who got in a car wreck, and one day he was really struggling, really struggling, drooling, and couldn't move his hand. Finally he knocked down the whole board. The young man looked at Bill, and he said: Bill, don't be embarrassed. You see this hand, that's trembling and shaking, my hand used to shake just like yours. And see, I can move these checkers.[30]

Hey, have you ever thought of how terribly young the world is? It could last thousands of more uncounted years, and then we and all our problems would seem so small.[31]

All of a sudden I wake up and this isn't vacation anymore. I am back in the working world, and I am destroying everything I had accomplished without even meaning to. I forget about it and step on it and the work crumbles. I drop a heavy wrong-shaped word on it and smash! The structure is gone that took years to build.

I feel a gush of wind. I am alone here. Boy, it's lonely to be a miracle.

I gasp but I can't do anything. It's a game of pick-up sticks. It took me 14 or 15 years to build that sand castle and now that the wave has dissolved it back into the sea, I can do nothing but look sideways at the hollow where it stood on the damp sand. There is no way that I can catch the damp grains disappearing into the vast stadium of sand, a countless number like the stars. There is nothing to do but to begin to build it again in the hollow where I stand right now.

Life is officially less simple than the black line that people tend to draw between life and death.

I think that's what the book of Ecclesiastes is about.

30. Brock, interview.
31. Wishful thinking in my journal.

Today, SHE IS

I am unbearably happy that this is me that this has happened to—not someone older with a settled brain, not someone younger with a more tender brain. My brain is in the one sweetspot of age that can even for hope for recovery.

I talk and talk and talk — way too much, way more than I mean to, far more than I want to, far more than I can. The only time I can actually think and communicate is when I write. Dorothy Sayers once again saves me. "Perhaps he's shy," suggests Phoebe Tucker, kindly, in *Gaudy Night*. "People who talk a lot often are."[32]

We used to laugh a lot at ourselves, because of the silly things. We'd laugh about the silly things that I had to do, that I had to learn — sometimes we would just have the best laughs in the whole world, just on us — she pauses, turns, shakes her head, holds the pause like a rubato — we chuckle every now and then, but we've probably done every silly thing you can do.[33]

All the same, I am so curious: Why didn't I get out of the way? Was I a hero protecting Mary Claire and Margot as much as I could? Or did I just have exceptionally slow reflexes, even then? Even when I could not even see through the fog of comatose, the question stuck in my mind like a thorn.

Why didn't I move? Was it half-baked heroism or exceptionally slow reflexes? It doesn't matter. I've broken no bones. I've broken my head. I've broken statistics. Most people die in trauma like this; most people don't recover consciousness from this kind of trauma; most people don't progress beyond a vegetative state after an "accident" like this; most survivors don't recover a high school degree; but most people — apparently? Or not? — aren't me.

32. Sayers, *Gaudy Night*, 36.
33. Brock, interview.

PART III

I asked him something about the word feeling — his response was, "I have no feeling. I have no feeling." Emotionally he just — he isn't there. It doesn't seem to bother him. He was a very high-strung, Type A personality. I've asked him so many times over the years what I can do for him to make him happier. . . and he says, I am content. How many people can say I am content, and really mean it? And he really means it. He is content.[34]

A poem of Paul Verlaine plays through the Autumn French classes at Carroll like Frederic Chopin's Raindrop Prelude. *Blessent mon Coeur . D'une langeure. Monotone.* "Chanson D'Autumne."[35] Looking out the window, feeling the rain in my heart as it pattered on the round, the coldness slips in the edges and slides down to a dark well, and I know just how he feels when his feelings shred his heart.

I catch glimpses of the heels of Molly Before-the-Accident only in the words of ancients, proofs that thousands have read. Midway in the journey of our life I found myself in a dark wood, said Dante Alighieri[36] — I had almost thought the words were said by St. Augustine — for I had fallen asleep and wandered from the straight path. That was a line I fell in love with last spring, before this happened.

Give me my scallop-shell of quiet. A line of Sir Walter Raleigh's ringing 600 years after his head rolled in a world that is still churning.[37]

C.S. Lewis wrote that to love at all is to be vulnerable.[38] I am alive. But to be alive is to be vulnerable.

---

34. Brock, interview.
35. Verlaine, "Chanson d'Automne."
36. Dante, *Part I: The Inferno*, 1:1.
37. Raleigh, "The Passionate Man's Pilgrimage."
38. Lewis, *The Four Loves,* 121.

PART IV

SHE IS IN THE back room when I come, I hear her shutting cabinets. She shuffles out briskly, Rosie snuffling at her heels. Oh, hello. Says Cinda. Ready?

I follow her into the music room, sit at the piano, accidentally kick the dog who nips my heel from underneath the piano bench. Time for the lesson.

I open my eyes and look at the wall. What has happened to me now, I want to know. I feel like I've been hit by a boat. Everything hurts. My grimace hurts my cheekbones and my eyes fill with tears and my throat is too swollen to fit air. I feel like I've been flattened out by a steamroller like a shapeless stretch of earthworm on an asphalt road, and patched together again and puffed back into the shape of a person.

Oh yes, aha, ahaha, I laugh to myself because this is funny, this is really funny — if I feel like I've been hit by a boat, that's because I have been hit by a boat. It hurts, it hurts, everything hurts, even the bones in my toes and the nerves in my ears. I lap up the breath-taking throb like a decadent poet taking absinthe, like a vampire with blood dripping down his jowls, in the sick way of an epicurean sucking the breath of life from an experience. I can't stop tearing into it, ripping it apart and concentrating on it,

PART IV

focusing on it, setting my eyes on it like a dog given a raw red beefsteak and gazing at it like a cross. Pain is real.

I don't want my plans to change. Maybe I won't minor in music like I thought, but I will still study it.

She doesn't yell but her thoughts are acid and I dread what she will think aloud in sharp, acerbic slices of a different life. Right hand, left hand, unison. It is so syrupy slow to draw the line between the notes on the paper and my fingers; I can draw the line, but my fingers don't obey when they hear me. I yell at them and there they are, sitting and wagging their tails until at last my index finger begins and the rest follow. I am tromping over the keys like a group of boys in heavy boots, tripping over themselves and unsure who led and who followed, drowning each other out.

Every morning, roll up the corners of the map of my mind. Tack the corners to the rotting corkboard and repeat as the corners curl down and the cartography crumples to the floor.

I put on mascara on eyes without life and despise myself for painting a manikin of myself in an attempt to disguise death-warmed-over. I walk mechanically but I can't imagine running. I can't live, I am so tired, and I can't sleep because I am already dead with eyes wired open. I have never experienced, never imagined anything like that kind of fatigue. It doesn't come ordinarily. It is physical, mental, spiritual, engrossing every sense and deadening life.

The day is dead, a grey piece of roadkill, indefinite and indecipherable. Søren Kierkegaard says that the specific character of despair is precisely this: it is unaware of being despair. Walker Percy responds that only once in my life was the grip of everdayness broken: when I lay bleeding in a ditch.[1] Nothing breaks it now but disaster and if I encounter

---

1. Percy, *The Moviegoer*, Epigraph, 145.

Today, SHE IS

another hard edge I will disintegrate like a sand sculpture. What holds me together now is the lack of wind.

Piano is something that I will continue, forever. Before, it was a hobby that I enjoyed, it was a me-thing. Now, it is therapy.

It goes on.

She is acerbic. No beating around the bush for Cinda. Her words are a rap across my knuckles. I *know* I got it wrong. I know my fingers should be faster — but they can't. It's like wading through waist-deep water to play this Baroque fugue or whatever it is. Reading two separate lines of music to translate through separate hands into the movements of distinct fingers on certain keys and not others — well we'll see how this goes. It's information dripping from my mind like a slow leaky faucet. Well get it right next time, says Cinda, clearly dissatisfied. She is happy to see the next student.

I read that Annie Dillard says that life — or land — or something, is a poured thing, and time a surface film lapping and fringeing at fastness.[2] Is this what King David means when he groans that he is poured out like water?[3] That he can't walk, can't think — that the world has degenerated into the dull mudded silt of chaos?

Frankly, all I want is for the phone to stop ringing and for people to stop asking about me. I don't want one more person to know how I am sleeping, how I am eating, how my body is functioning, whether or not I have my period back yet, whether or not I am tired or limping or my eyes are alert. They aren't. That's life. It's dead. They — all of they — feel like they own a little piece of my health because the whole world was involved with bringing me back to life. I

2. Dillard, *Holy the Firm*, 21.
3. Ps. 22:14.

PART IV

understand that, but I want me, too. I am scraped skint and barely here. There is no life to share.

Head-ache says Cinda. She retreats to the back room, lesson over.

"I'm alright, thanks," I say, "I'm great." "I'm fine."

Oh, God! What do they want me to say? How do they think I am? I was run over by a boat and I feel like I was run over by a boat. I am losing my mind and I can't function. I'm so godlessly cold, all the time, all the time, and motionless, and emotionless. What I do feel is pain. I'm going to reply, "I'm great!" with as many exclamation points as I can fit into one sentence because I know it comforts them to ask. Just, please, please, don't ask further, because I hate to lie through my teeth.

Give me this pain like a drug to tell me that I live and these appendages are mine. It belongs to me and I rustle away mastership. I don't pretend to be the captain of my shipwreck but this, this I can own. The back of my brain drowns out the yammering and all is still because all I can hear is a heavy death metal band having a reunion in my head. I get up and begin the day but I hunch my right shoulder like a cripple and my head is jerking and tilted like a marionette. Take off the ribbon and away it will roll. My mouth is pressed and my eyes squint like they are thinking hard. That's the day. Just today. Ladies, Gentleman, allow me to introduce Pain. Usher it in on the arm of your shiny black suitcoat, give it your elbow like an attentive groomsman; escort it, and let it run wild like a drunken socialite pouncing on a party. Let it pound through me and shred my insides so that I can't look past it into tomorrow.

Can flavorless food be eaten without salt?[4]

---

4. Job 6:6.

Today, SHE IS

"Ya-all," maybe she'll say, "Ma-am. Did you wear smocked dresses drinking lemonade on your porch? *Miss* Cinda!"

I used to have blue eyes but now they are flat as a piece of matte black construction paper.

"DebYouSee," she calls my favorite composer in odd flat syllables, "Claude Debussy." The room turns blue and spins into a Van Gogh painting when she plays Debussy however. Miss Cinda plays the world feelingly.[5]

There is always the other hand. When I am so happy I can't take it. When I am so overwhelmed by something beautiful that I cry and can't help it. But more and more the cavern inside of me deepens. I am desperately trying to patch it before it is a gulf but there are no memories to caulk the holes. My emptiness is awkward and gaping, a black hole that I want to cover up with a blouse, with lipstick, with something pretty — but then a button pops. Something shows.

Now what? I think I have accidentally slipped into the wrong party — I missed the day I was supposed to die, and now I am hanging on awkwardly, not sure whether to go on or go back, in between conversations at an otherwise lively dinner party.

She is sharper and she speaks like a lemon, sourly, but I don't mind. I can tell that she has a headache. Her head is about to roll off too. She plays and it is as light as a helium balloon and I wish we could just both float away and continue forever in Debussy and Chopin, Miss Cinda playing on her full grand and both of us happy and light-headed. But now it is my turn.

---

5. Shakespeare, *King Lear*, 4:6.

PART IV

Footsteps up and to the ground. Footsteps up and to the ground but it has changed. There is a hole. There is a rock. The ground looks farther away than it is and perhaps I am so close to that tree that I will jar my arm, like I just did. This is a landscape that I am not a part of.

I am about to fall to the ground because I am not tired but I am panting; I am not worn out but my body can't move any farther so I will pull it along very slowly, by a string. I can feel my right knee twittering and twinging in and out of its socket, muttering that I don't treat it well and there is no such thing as gratitude these days. My knee is 9 dog years, which is 63 in human terms, and if I don't hold on to it I am scared that it will fall right off, like an arm from a sleeve or trousers from legs.

For her sister and her nephews Cinda has a real soft spot. They're her family, and she loves them. Her parents irritate her but she loves those boys. I am irritating to teach, I know. I drive myself crazy, she doesn't know. The tumor is taking over the room, I can tell, and I sit and I smile and I try again, methodically following an exercise in self-control, self-humiliation. At this point it is self-flagellation. I can't do it and so I will hurt myself, drumming the fact of a misconditioned brain in through my fingers. That should do the trick.

Again I have the feeling. . . I don't belong here. If I am dead, why can't I sail over it, flow through it like a ghost? This world doesn't want me. The rocks are jagged and point at me like knives and the trees watch like armed guards that will rip me if I come too close.

The ground is uncertain, a woven mat with strategically placed pit-falls. Pine straw, I love the pine straw that homes chipmunks, but it is mischievous, piled fifteen feet high like a haystack you can't see, and it will slip away with

Today, SHE IS

you like a magic carpet if you don't watch out and take your knee cap with it while the rest of your calf jerks behind like the leg of a marionette.

All I have to remember is to connect my feet to the ground.

I sit playing piano, scales up and scales down, the same scales but different every time because of the places my fingers go. Tick-tock-tick-tock-tick-tock-tick . tick . tick . tick . tick . tick . This is a great occupation for a musician on the verge of insanity. But aren't they all?

Hours playing up and playing down.

My fingers crumble. I do nothing but practice and my heart is withering because of my ineptitude but this is my punishment and I am forcing myself to carry it out because . this . will . help . at . last. I remember my exceptional trills of yore I don't say as my third and fourth finger stumble on the keys like Irish dancers who have been lamed and can't speed up to save their skins.

I feel every brain signal darting through my head with the burn of a laser beam as it carries the black note for every finger from the page to the keyboard and my immobilized fingers creak out the door on the lonely dirt path to producing music.

I play to have a conversation with my soul — but neither the soul nor the conversation is there.

3:00 a.m. It is sometime in March, 2003. I am sixteen.

The house is pitch tar and there are no stars, no rush of wind outside. The light in the bathroom is a dirty cream glare in my eyes. The girl in the mirror terrifies me. Her flat black eyes tell me what I have been afraid to admit to myself. I am dead, she says. This is my secret. The only secret I have left to hide is this: there is no soul. I trust in God, but I can't see any enlightenment in the blackness of my mind or

PART IV

any self beneath this facade. All that I am is written on my pasty-ill white face and my black-button eyes.

2:57 a.m. 3:26 a.m. 3:57 a.m. She scares me because she shows no emotion — none whatsoever — on seeing me. Her face is blank, and her eyes are a dark, flat shade of no-color. The iris is black more than anything else. The cheeks are drab to a degree not skin-toned, dark gray pits beneath her eyes. Hair is sparse, lips much too large and abnormally swollen in the harsh bathroom light.

The voice is coming from the dark gray pits in which they are buried in coffins; the pupils larger-than-life bulge out to speak the truth. They are talking even though they are dead. This is it, they say. This is it. This is what you can expect to see at 4:11 a.m. every night of your life. Here they are now, and here they will always be.

I catch them in the corner of my eye and I shudder and want to run at first because there should not be another person awake at this time of night and I know there should not be a stranger in the bathroom with me. I force myself to confront the image and find my face in the mirror but not myself: this person is dead.

Kaboom. Boom. Boom.

In my head vibrating like the echoes in a vacant metal silo, the cold air poundered by the mallet thwacking the side of the round shed in an even staccato.

Truth walks through me like I am a ghost and trails the bitter reality behind it like a mocking prank.

I am a ghost. My soul is gone. My life stopped on July 27th, 2002, under a speedboat. These are the shreds that were peeled off, neither alive nor dead. I am living out the coma. In between, apathetic, and in netherness. I am eeking out a life that stopped. They saved my body though I can't feel it, but my soul is gone.

Today, SHE IS

I force myself to face the ghost in the bathroom mirror. This is now and this is then. Selah, I whisper.

Cold, cold as death. Rigor mortis is the state of frozen bodies, soulless and motionless. The chill of indifference paralyzes your bones.

The rising sun of the morning unhinges the mask and I do not even believe it anymore. I need emotion to thaw my frozen body from this rigor mortis. I scavenge for it like an almost-dead thing in a dying world, a survivor from a world calamity digging for scant forest roots like the crazed woman in the wood of a horror film. My dirt-filled fingernails are broken and jagged and all I have is one miniscule shard of a dead sprout from the vast entire forest to keep me alive, a wish-bone frail pinky-twig of desire but the minuscule thing is crumbling as I think, and I drop what is left back in the pit that it came from.

Over and over and over and over, that face terrifies me, a stranger's head wearing my clothes. I am so numb I can't feel my body. It's like losing the love of your life. He's gone and you're here, but where is your body. You can't feel it — you touch it, but it's not there, and so you cradle it and squeeze it to know that the nerves in your brain are attached to this thing. I look in the mirror at a husk that terrifies me, a husk wearing a pink sweater with nothing inside of it. Nothing.

Emptiness. All head, a swollen balloon-sized head carrying a war inside of it, peopled with a world of its own like *Horton Hears a Who*,[6] about to burst out of its shell wearing a mask so that it can frequent the living room like a human person and not scare the children like the face of the Phantom of the opera house, half-devil.

---

6. Suess, *Horton Hears a Who!*.

PART IV

    Beat against it as I will, there is nothing. I try to revive it like a doctor saving a dying person but no breath of feeling responds. I stare at the mirror into apathetic death.

    I slam the door and I sit against it shuddering, wishing with my heart that I could be honestly enraged. Dare I tell them — anyone — I will not tell myself — that I only have these scenes to pretend that I can feel. This is what the normal person would feel so I will act out the scene like a bad actress, a vamp with too much rouge and overpouffed sticky red lips and perhaps a wig trailing over her ample bosom except mine is not worth mentioning. I am freezing with non-feeling. Let me boil myself in rage and let anger wash this apathy away. I am over-powered by the fingers of icy cold clawing me, clawing my veins with venom and not the hot cathartic formula a good tantrum should give. Get it away from me, I shudder, cut these feelings off of me — but they stroke me clammily and hold, lightly, tightly, like the fingers of a pervert. Forever. Forever. Forever.

    I feel dead. I act dead. I could take the lifeless acting. Even though I can't sleep they say I should get healthier and eventually I may even walk without walking into walls. But not the lifeless feeling, the no-care presses down on me and the world drips metal-gray paint. Let me walk through walls. I am a dead soul trapped in a body: what good can I do here when I can't even talk because sleep is drowning my brain and anti-seizure drugs cloy my mouth like a hand holding down my tongue.

    And inside, the gray flat poison says in monotone, sometime you will have to get up and stand back to the wall, showing a face to a world that will never change. And neither will you. You will paint the lips too wide stained red with the tips pointed on your cheekbones so that they will not see you will not know you will not know that your neck

Today, SHE IS

is strangled by degrees by the tilt of your chin as your black eyes stare.

"What are they waiting for?" I remember Daddy saying, exasperated by a couple who is spending years of their lives in a state of engagement. "Life happens in the meantime." Recovery isn't a matter of climbing, continuously.

Recovery is a matter of accepting that now is forever.

Life happens in the meantime.

You try to love — I try to love and I think that I do. Sometimes I am overwhelmed by it. "She's in love," they say, "Daddy, Ariel's in love."[7]

There isn't any doubt as to why I am here. I am a miracle, and what are miracles? They are supernatural sign posts enacted by God for those who ask for them. There is this Latin verse that I've always loved. Who knows where it comes from. *Lux umbra Dei*: light is the shadow of God.[8]

Cinda and I play Be Thou My Vision together for my senior recital. That's a tear, I think. It is — she wipes it away.

The desert before me is vast, shapeless and shifting in the breeze with no footprints for my feet to fit into and follow. My place in the world was expunged by a tide and I am bryophyta nicheless, a three-quarter oyster shell on the wet shore. Now nothing breaks it—but disaster. Only once in my life was the grip of everdayness broken: when I lay bleeding in a ditch. Walker Percy, *The Moviegoer*.[9] The loss of blood from a skinned knee is too much for me to bear.

Cinda is dying. Her brain tumor is back in remission. I go to see her at her parents' house — she remembers me, it is six months but 30 years later. We talk of old movies,

---

7. *The Little Mermaid*. Dir. Clements/Musker, Walt Disney Pictures.

8. 18th c. sundials, Gloucester, UK.

9. Percy, *The Moviegoer*, 145.

PART IV

Hollywood grace, Grace Kelly, Cary Grant — suddenly we are bonded by love and a fellowship of pain, by romance in black-and-white, Debussy, bad trills, by bad things that happen in your brain. Ebby moans in the corner. What were we talking about? Asks Cinda. Yes! You have to come again.

I pick up C.S. Lewis' *A Grief Observed*. *The act of living is different all through. Her absence is like the sky*, he says, *it is spread over everything*.[10]

Magnanimous despair alone could show me so divine a thing, breathed Andrew Marvell.[11]

There is this beautiful book of poetry by Linda Pastan that I skimmed. The last lines snag my eyes and hold them: *It caught me. I finally reach it. But something is wrong. Grief is a circular staircase. I have lost you*.[12] The girl crushed in a bizarre freak accident on July 27, 2002 is not here. Is it legitimate to grieve for yourself? My parents did not give me life but they gave me love. I am here for love of their love. That is a place. There aren't any single contexts left, now.

Whoever would have his life must lose it. When Sir Andrew Marvell wrote that magnanimous despair alone could show him so divine a thing, he was speaking of love — but love, death, life — they are so translucent that at some point near the end of July 2002, the definitions slipped through my fingers with French and algebra.

---

10. Lewis, *A Grief Observed*, 24.
11. Marvell, "The Definition of Love."
12. Pastan, "The Five Stages of Grief."

PART V

A wicked and adulterous generation asks for a sign! But none shall be given it except the sign of the prophet Jonah.[1]

MY MIND IS WRITING a work of historical fiction about my past. So far, it is a collection of sentences, first lines that agree with the stories recalled by the mind of someone else.

But today, my mind writes, I am six years old, awake before the rest of the house, spending the first vacation morning at Mere's house by walking around the edge of the well. And then — I fall into the slimy green water, deeper than I thought it was, and terrify the huge goldfish. I am wet-through with the green mineral water, yammering on the porch for someone to open the door for me. I don't want to get the floor wet.

This memory is mine.

My past is growing in photographs again like a watercolor paint-by-number kit.

My eyelids pop and just waked, I look around. I was not asleep and my eyes were not closed but what was I

---

1. Matt. 12:39.

PART V

doing one instant before this time. I have no idea. None, whatsoever. This happens a lot. The pop, the instant of recognition and the realization that I was not asleep but that I have no memory of that moment before.

Did you ever see *The Fly*. It's something in between *The Blob* and Hitchcock, and concerns a scientist who misfires his experiment and turns himself into a fly. The really poignant scene of the movie is when his wife is looking for him and the scientist-fly is screaming in agony but she can't hear him, no one can hear him.[2]

Sometimes I blink because no one else hears the Fly shrieking in my head. I know just how Jack, the dog feels. A whisper falls in my ear like shattered glass. For no reason something is wrong and my right ear is pounding me for hurting it. I'm sorry, I didn't mean to. I gasp — Just a sudden twinge, that's all, I'm okay.

The twinges snap in and snap out. Better than the days when I can't hear at all and I swim through my head to register the scene in front of me; like looking in the glass of an aquarium, the peripheral does not exist. Usually we look into the aquarium; from here, I am looking out, trying to lip-read what they are saying but I am so bad at it. Sorry, I yell, I have a cold, a bad cold. Yeah, a really bad cold!

Vomit crawls up my throat like a lizard up a doorframe, vile and more repulsive than any healthy flu nausea. It is one of those needle-hooks of a rejected experience, to paraphrase *Brideshead Revisited*,[3] like the bit of gilding, the tone of a clock's striking, the certain smell that recalls one to a tragedy — but I can't place the tragedy. I don't know what it is recalling me to — and then, and then, it tacks a picture in my brain. I know how I know this place.

2. *The Fly*. Dir. Kurt Neumann.
3. Waugh, *Brideshead Revisited*, 164.

Today, SHE IS

This is the vomit of a rejected experience before the sickly breeze of bamboo. I pop my ear through an awkward crack of the neck.

I open my eyes, although they haven't been closed, and I look at my hands, which are holding — beads. My arms are asleep and my legs are asleep. Actually, my whole body is asleep and my head is awkwardly jammed on my shoulder. I shake my head. Wake up, please wake up, please, please, please wake up. I slip the beads onto the string but I can't see them anymore and I have to keep re-stringing them.

He has dark eyes, black eyes, expressionless and pitiless and relentlessly they fix me. I will not be held. This time that I start I look down and see a pattern that I don't remember stringing.

I turn. There he is, across the room, a room full of people. I enter into the throng; they will camouflage me so he will never find me. And so I do, and so I disappear into the midst of people and I am talking, lifting my glass, when I catch his eye. His intent eyes have never left me. I turn to hide again but there he is, at my elbow, owning me. I try to slip away but, very gently he does not allow it. He just stands there, holding me while I watch the crowd of safety wave goodbye one by one and the pit in my stomach is so strong that I almost throw up and the nausea is choking me in my throat.

We are always in that room, a room like an Elk's Lodge, largish, not too clean, all wooden rustic logs. And he always wins. I am checkmated. I start, look around me.

I always imagined Nineveh as a city in the wind and dust of the desert from the walls, but with the glamour and Wal-Mart glaze of Vegas within the terra cotta walls, voluptuous fat Revlon-lipped blonde beauties in shiny top hats

PART V

and skanky black vests and fish net tights shimmying up columns at every corner. The men are cold and dull, politicians, bankers, always in parliaments concocting cruel torturements before they stop with the porch beauties on their ways home to neglect their wives and torture their slaves.

It's like a breeze came in from the closed door to a completely quieted room, and I smell cold bamboo that washes that taste down my throat. It is so much worse than vomit that I want to choke but I don't, instead I roll my head and try to crack my neck for relief. Or maybe I don't, I just imagine that I do because I am walking into a log cabin with a wet bar and the room is full of people; I have been here before, I know, I recognize it, this is where I come when I black out before this world vanishes from my mind like a withdrawn spell. I know it is him though I honestly can't say even at this moment what he looks like, what he is wearing, but I know that his eyes find me and fixate on me and that even now he is trying to maneuver me out on my own. I move this way and he moves that, a sniper, I move from his range of fire and he moves me back into it, around until I am cornered and we are moving out of the door.

I go to find my sister but I can't be around people. I play the piano but I can't take the racket in my ears and I am too tired to read music and translate it through my fingers. I turn on music but I can't take a beat, I turn on a book on cd but I can't take the voice. I drink a mug of coffee in a gulp and all I can think of is Khazad Dum, pound pound pound, because my head is on fire and so big that it will swell and topple off and roll away — and my body is tiny, so tiny a cat could catch it like a mouse, and its gentle paws would rip it apart. I want to curl up in silence and forget this. I curl up and the silence screams at me; the night begins. I don't want that. I cannot be alone because he will be there. It cannot be night because the night will last forever, forever, always night and never sleep.

And Jonah — Jonah is a sign, a bearded sign under force. He did not want to bring salvation. At first he refused to tell the Ninevites that God would forgive their lasciviousness and Platonic cruelty before He would destroy them for their ways. He refused to say what God told him to declare, and so he was salted by the sea and gulped down the stinking gullet of a gentile fish and, three days later, spat out onto the briny sand, a symbol of salvation to the sailors of Tarshish.

I blink. I am standing on a stepladder in the bathroom reaching for something on the top shelf of the cabinet and I blink. I was about to fall, when I blinked. Hold a piece of black paper in your right hand. Slide it behind your eyes: you see what I saw.

I have no idea what is in my hand, no idea what is the time, no idea — literally, no idea — in my mind. I climb down. I don't know why I am holding this, or what I was reaching for. I feel ill, I am about to faint, and I taste the acidity and the rancor of despair in my mouth and I smell bamboo and I know, I know it, that he asked me to get what I was reaching for. It is a certainty like despair that he did. If I needed proof, then I have it — it would be in the rancid nausea drowning my tongue.

It feels very, very late at night and it is dark down here, but I hear voices upstairs and I scuffle up the stairs. There is a dinner party going on. That's right. Oh God, thank you that I have not been here days.

This is so weirdly magical. I slide into the evening like I haven't been missed, have not been gone, like I lead a seamless double life that I cling to because I can feel him,

PART V

in the background, snipping threads and ripping out the seams. He wants in; he wants me out.

Is he real? I don't want this backward upside down to be reality. Is it not? I don't want myself to be always half-in, half-out of reality — not even that, to be overtaken by a dream world that I can't escape. This is a game that I can't win. Let it be real and let me be lost in this wasteland. Let it not be real — I would give my life for it not to be real — and I can't tell the difference between the map of my mind and the topography of life. You know other words for people like that, you know other places for them — you've seen them walking down the street, muttering to the devil on their shoulder in a reality that we are not a part of while you and I are hazed into an uncomfortable background.

Three days in the cavern of bones, three days in Hell before God brought the prophet out into the world of sunshine, a living testament of God's grace and care in every detail in the life of a single cantankerous man, an ornery old prophet who brought salvation to the city of more than a hundred and twenty thousand Ninevite souls and became a monument of wonder like Lot's salted wife to the readers of Scripture and the consumers of the Bible-infested Western economy.

Why am I so brave? Why can I take this? This is my life. In most cases, there is no fear of the known.

In the in-between state, yes, I am white with terror; but in one or the other, I live. This is the point where I began to develop an awkward, involuntary gulp that sounds like Gollum's gollum.

Oh, God. I cry in straits.

I find myself alone with him. Forget about the people, the foreplay, let him circle me in the log room.

Today, SHE IS

If that was it I could take it. It's the taste, the taste of terror, the taste of Hell running up my throat and licking the roof of my mouth dry, that makes the pit drop from my stomach like a brick.

The prostitutes, the decadents, the Ninevites saw the sign of Jonah and believed.

Today I am in a crowded street, loads of people walking by, quickly, nothing to catch my eye. Someone calls my name and I turn around to wave at a friend but on the turn I caught him, in the corner of my eye, watching me.

Word came to the king of the Nineveh and he rose from his throne and laid aside his robe; he wound himself with sackcloth, and he scattered himself with ashes. The king declared the imminent destruction and called every man and every woman to mourn with him: God relented from the disaster that He had said He would bring upon them.

I pick my leg up awkwardly and it falls because the ground is so much closer than it looks. I slip against the wall and kebang my whole side is bruised. I thought this was a pool party. I smelled the chlorine as I slipped into the water. I know the people here, they're in swimsuits; it's sunny; there's a cabana and it is so warm that I don't mind. Oh God, oh God, oh God, there is soap in my hair. There is steam stoking the bathroom and I am in the shower. I must have been here for hours, lying on the floor.

The shower. this is. dangerous. I sleep with my mom because I can't keep my head from falling off when I come out because I am so tired so tired so tired. After I climb between the sheets and let my head spin I wake up, instantly, I am somewhere else, I wake up, instantly, I am here in bed, I wake up, instantly, I am not here, I wake up, instantly, I am in bed with my mother for the whole, night, long, not

PART V

sleeping but waking up, again and again and again, seconds, instants apart, worse than Groundhog Day.[4] And all day long it is the same, and the next and the next and the next. The involuntary gollum in my throat continues to almost strangle me but my neck twists strangely and saves me.

I don't think that this is the time to tell my parents, to tell them that, most of the time, actually, or some of it, a small big part of the time, I am seeing things that are not actually around me, and that most of the people that I interact with, most of the conversations that I have, are not actually happening. I'm already taking so many of the right anti-depressant, anti-hallucinatory drugs that don't work anyway and I can't purposefully change again. Changing drugs is hard on me. It's hard on my parents. It's hard on everyone.

But I am going to see the psychologist. I prepare myself, resignation. I crave escape.

Jonah sat in the bitter sun and shriveled like the plant that grew beside him. Did he never believe in the salvation that he himself was a sign of? We don't know.

When I find out that this is just a regular old assessment I hold in my tears and cry bitterly when I am alone in my room at home.

Idiot.

!
!

There is no exit from your own mind.

I wake up into an upside down world. What is so new about that? What kind of world do you expect it to be at 6:18 a.m. when you didn't fall asleep until an ungodly hour

4. *Groundhog Day*, Dir. Ramis.

Today, SHE IS

you don't even remember? I can't open my eyes because I hurt so much, all over, and when they open, the fog doesn't roll up the coast like it should to pave the way for a bright morning.

I sit up into a cloud of burn in my head and I feel my way through it as gingerly as I can, walking is as hard as running up a hill in snow.

The bathroom door creaks and there are my sisters, braiding pigtails, brushing teeth. Get ready, get ready! Ski day! I love skiing! I love skiing! It's a pipsqueaking chant. Pulling on heavy wool socks, eating oatmeal, packing lunches. My brother has already packed the car before we go upstairs. *Kyrie elaison*.

My head weighs as much as a bowling ball, I carry so much pain in it, but what can you do. I've dosed as much as I can. I always dose as much as I can. You can get nauseous from Tylenol and coffee you know, and you can definitely get a migraine.

Ski day. I drink the coffee and the acid burns behind my eyes like a laser, but I will be ready for ski day. I will go now that I won't have a seizure. I make myself.

When we arrive the wind is evil, sharp. The colors are wrong, glaring at me, lasering through my eyes. The hill is a field of ice, smooth as a pane of glass, jarred by rocks and branches sticking out in places. I am so cold. It's warm today! Isn't it warm today! Isn't it hot today? They say. I am so cold that my tongue sticks to the roof of my mouth. Damnation. Bloody Hell.

Yes, haha! I laugh to them. I don't want to ski but it is the last day of my first season back. It's been a year. A year and a half. Almost two. That pre-accident girl I've heard about *loved* to ski.

Watch out, watch out. What is she doing up here like a red cherry puffball, she is so small, so small in this Antarctic

PART V

glacier of ice and rock. What has health to do with care? Health has to do with carelessness, with not caring, not fearing, not feeling.

Yes, I say to him over my shoulder, yeah, yeah! I say and nod and look at all the people at this party, I converse, and I look around me. It looks like I am in a movie scene. The wind is whipping my eyes to shreds and tears are trickling to my goggles. Then my eyes roll open.

Dear Jesus Christ — There is no way to stop racing on a sheet of ice down a mountain. I shouldn't be going this fast and I can't stop. Molly, they yell, Molly stop they all waited at the top of the hill but I went right over and bang. Bang. Bang.

I open my eyes. I am awake once more. Here I am, stopped, jackknifed by a pine. I am bent double, crumpled by a pine, my skis are buried in a heap of snow. I can't believe that I can walk on these knees. I can't believe that bones can hurt this much without being broken. Oh, oh, oh God, dear God in heaven, what just happened. What just happened.

No use waiting here, I follow. They are all squatting down on their skis in a line like ducks. I am racing down the hill, when I come to and open my eyes. I have no idea where I have been or what I have been doing. I am awake just in time to crest over the icy hill and tumble down spread eagle. A rocks rip into my back. Did that just happen. The world is spinning. I am so dizzy that I cannot stand up. Did that just happen. Where was I? Who cares about the rock. Where have I been — that's all that I want to know. What was I thinking? I didn't do anything stupid. I honestly have no memory of the past five minutes. Where were my eyes?

I wake up. I wake up. The hill is sliding past. I wake up. Gulp, stay with it Molly! Focus. I focus. The people ahead of me are in a video game and I am playing it, directing myself. They are all in a video game, falling and laughing but not people.

I can watch this. I can play this too. The hill is sliding past. I am focused. The hill is sliding past and boy, I am with it.

I wake up before I trip. Head over heels. Tumble down and my feet are above my head, just like a somersault, skitips buried. Good, good heavens. I don't remember the last ten minutes. No memory. Just blank. The last time the hill slid past I was not here.

I just keep skiing. That is all I know how to do. I am a shell and I go. Now that I can ski, I will ski. This is Forever, keeps running through my mind, written in pen on a tag dropped on the street before every step, written in letters of smoke by an aeroplane in the empty blue sky of my mind. This is the meantime: this is forever. Your real life drowned and now you have a play, a play of life, so play at ski.

I . am . going . to . kill . myself. Not on purpose, and that is the really ironic part. Because as much as I would like to, I will not touch myself. I am sacred because I lived and if you lay a hand against a holy vessel, you will surely die. What is more sacred than something set apart by God?

This is the rule in this video game that I can't break. I am going to kill myself through my own stupidity, my own incapacity. I am going to die a horrible, stupid, stupid death — one of those deaths you read about and think, *what an idiot*! *What a waste*!

I am only saltily glad that my hand will be the one to do it and that it will probably not take long to happen.

I ski down the hill, all with it, watching the tracks before me, deeply ingrained into the snowbank. And then I watch nothing, a blank screen, and when I wake up face down in the snow I have no idea where I have been or how long I have been there. Damn, damn, dam-na-tion.

PART V

It's like that old movie with Gregory Peck, *Spellbound*.[5] He made a gorgeous amnesiac.

One more time. This has all been on one run; but we are almost to the bottom. Fry, fry, fry again. Bravely I confront a powderless sheet of ice and follow it down, with it for the most part, there are flashes here and there where I am not. And then over the crest of the hill I come to. Slow down, they are shouting, yelling but, really, I can't hear them. Over the crest of the hill I come to: what am I doing. Where have I been.

A memory slips through my mind like a panel, there and gone, just a face, no expression, slipping through as I slide sideways over the crest and tumble down the hill with my knees odd directions. I come to looking at the sky with my feet uphill and I remember that face. Oh God, I gulp, involuntarily, and almost throw up but I am going too fast. I remember it because I've been seeing it all morning, in the in between times, and I know that that is where I have been. I know his expressionless malice. He is luring me, trying to keep my eyes on him until the last minute when he pushed me over the crest. God, God, this is not safe. I will kill someone else if I don't kill myself.

Today he is malicious. A devil. When he lures me away he doesn't lure me, he makes the move — he approaches me and keeps me until the last minute when he spins me and lets me go and I crash. God, he is trying to kill me. He is, he is trying to kill me, he told me so with that laugh and that push.

I take off my skis and trip inside the lodge, which is a fishbowl, a humid fishbowl, people moving, staggering in surreally large clubfeet, bumping into me. Inside of me is a turmoil of warm nausea. If I sit down some motherly

---

5. *Spellbound*, Dir. Alfred Hitchcock.

person will want to talk. Huge log walls, the smell of melting sweat and stiff socks. Peace, peace, there is no peace. No rest for the wicked and no rest for me.

Hahaha, wasn't that an awesome day! They are all saying, all talking about the hilarious afternoon on the melting slopes. We were practically swimming that last hill.

Let's go home, can't we please go home. This is Forever. The waters surrounding me, drowning my soul, if I have one: there is not a breath of air. Not alive, and not dead: this netherworld is forever, and this netherworld is Hell, Hell on earth, Hell in your head.

THIS IS MY LIFE: I say. This is my life: the one reality that shaped everything, that shaped me and my future is an event that I am not aware of, that I don't remember. How characteristic. Ha.

At home that day at last, two and a half years from the day I was saved, is the first time that I pray for a miracle for myself. Our Father in Heaven, I ask, let this long winter be over. Make it spring. Make it morning again. Wake me up and let this be over. Let this not be life. Please, please, God, wake me up and let me dead: let me have died underneath that boat, drowned by the thousands of feet of dark-blue glacier-cold water like my life was drowned. Please make me wake up and this all be just a miraculously bad dream. Make me go back. Make me go back and be awake before the accident, dead before this happened.

I woke up and ten days and a lifetime had passed by. Why can't I do the same backwards? Oh, God, Our Father Who Art in Heaven, please, God! Please! Oh God, I beg, I beg, I beg You: please, let me wake up and be dead. Let me wake up two and a half years ago and let me die in a car accident the night before; let me be eaten by bears two weeks before. But please, let me be almost 15 ½ again — please, God, take this cup. I'm tired, let me go home.

PART V

Where is the adventure in this. Let it be over. I have tried and I have tried. I have been brave and I have been braver and I have done so much. God, please let the adventure be over. What is an adventure that you can never win. What kind of adventure has no hero — has a hero who always, always fails — no chance of success — not even an enemy to battle — just a circumstance, buried by a circumstance.

An adventure is a challenge is something that you can conquer, can succeed, if you overcome. There is no battling this; nothing to battle, I can only blame the accursed pleasure-seeker who I hope is reminded that he did not take the time to look for every day of his life like I am. His torture won't take my pain away. There is just this miraculous coffin that is stifling me oh so slowly, torturously, and I must be thankful for this coffin and give thanks that I can feel the weight of the dirt covering my coffin at my own burial while I weakly flail in my grave and the shovels of dirt fall on my coffin one, by, one, covered by flowers, pretty things, listening to praises that I am here to see how lovely this is.

So many people prayed for a miracle: I am the one who has to be thankful for it.

This prayer I know, I know, will only be answered one way. This prayer has already been prayed, and it has already been answered with a miracle. This tempest is for me. I am the answer. I am the miracle.

They call Stephen the first martyr. Hadn't Lazarus the rawer deal? Writes C.S. Lewis in a night of anguish; I am glad he has written it first.[6]

I don't ask it that day. I know that I can't or I will — not — be — happy, let's say. I know that I can't. I won't even go there because there is nothing, there is no reason not to. Still it's there in the back of my mind ricocheting with

6. Lewis, *A Grief Observed*, 53.

the batter of the cannon balls and the taste of nausea. I just know that I can't pick it out to pick apart and tempt myself. It is something I knew like I know that I must not respond to the bearded man who only wants me to talk to him: I just know.

There are not many facts in my life. I am already the freak, the one in a millionth survival story, and there isn't much to say about what my future looks like compared to similar stories. This tempest is for me. The novelty of certainty keeps me from temptation. I hold onto this fact and cradle the knowledge. It is sacred.

. . .

It is not the night. It is not the day. It is a netherworld at 3:00 a.m., blacker than either, ever, when I see a girl in the bathroom. Hard to say what color her hair is; her eyes are black. She is not alive. I lose my breath; I can't move for fear the ghost will move — talk to me — bite me — shadows move on the wall behind me. At last I can take it no longer and I move — what kind of world is this where up is down and the floor is ten feet deep? With an unspeaking shadow? What has she to say? She is dead.

She is dead — she is dead, I realize, and I know that the ghost is me. She drowned. This is clear at night, when she has no mind and her body is torturous and clubfoot like a Zombie. She — I — died. There is a sigh of relief. It explains why my body is drowning, by the minute, why my mind is nowhere to be found. She is dead. Let her rest in peace.

. . .

I have never — not when I was awake at least — been this bruised. Huge splotches, bright bright, bright blue like tropical fish, and green like Christmas lights and purple-black like dark cocoa, leopard-spot my legs and tattoo my

PART V

torso, even braceletting my upper arms and shoulders. My face is fine. A little ice-burned and scratched by the claws of the wind, that's all.

Over-dosing on pills really is not as easy as you think anyway. There was one disgusting story in a teen girl's magazine that was in my mind in particular, about a bulimic ex-suicide who failed her over-dose and had her stomach pumped and lived a painful time of not dying. All of those depressing doctor's office mags and dying waiting rooms at least were good for something. I'm sure the staff would be happy to know that they helped me to rule out over-dosing.

Out of one and into the next. My life is an accident I am beginning to feel. One bruise after the other. I fall dizzily out of bed or I walk into a door and get a goose egg in my forehead, that really hurt, or I crumple into a pine tree and fall down a ski slope. GOD, God, I pray though at this point it doesn't make any difference. I can't help it because I don't know what else to do and it is completely involuntary, a reflex reaction to the horror of the Marks-A-Lot green on my legs. Gollum.

Some night around this time the ghost of the girl comes back in the bathroom mirror of the netherhours, expressionleast. She has nothing to say but I think it is because of the Technicolor dream-coat bruised onto her body that the revelation falls on me like a stage curtain knocking me to the floor.

I am the sign of Jonah. I drowned underneath a boat, a speedboat, and now I'm back, a sign by default, a miracle who cannot declare. I had it all wrong: there is nothing I have to say to make a declaration. No worries about failing. I don't declare: I do declare. My being here is the miracle, I knew that: now I see that my body is the declaration, signed and sealed.

Today, SHE IS

I stand around them, I talk, I laugh, because I have to make believe that I can talk and laugh with people my age and ignore the chasmous depths whirling in blackness between us. I have developed a strange sort of talent. My mind is army-crawling through a thicket of thorns, trying for dear life to avoid the mines. I can't always. Sometimes I tap a tentacle that runs with a signal to the mine and off it goes and I crumple, hurtling down the crater that it leaves. I am huddled inside it wounded and gasping while my mouth ignores me, aping conversation and mouthing replies, intelligent or not as the mood calls. No ambulance hurtles to my aid because no one can see. I am that smart.

Written with a culture ravaged and slashed by rapacious Norsemen, Deor the Anglo-Saxon wrote that passed away, this also may.[7]

At this point I can't resist, but I am not wound, stressed, uptight anymore. God knows reality. I walk in that world, with them; talking to them. I am adept, a secret agent, I can snap in and out like a fox and fool everyone. I can respond to my brother, to the man on the street, in a seemly if slowing way. On the other side, I am more in that world with every step. I am so tired there is no resistance: it is as much as I can do to track with both and not to betray either. But I know that I drowned and I lived: I've seen salvation. That passed away, this also may.

I hold my coffee while it gets cold as I look out the window at the ancient poster-blue rocks shaded like faces. We get to Old Navy, we get to the mall and I am so tired that I can't pick up my feet; nothing to seize my fancy.

In the mirror I don't know whether this is my new sweater or my old one, but I don't like it so I shimmy out and slide it on the hanger while I'm in my bra. He doesn't say anything, whether he likes it or not. He puts his hand on

7. Deor, "Deor's Lament."

PART V

my shoulder and I stiffen. It is colder than me and already my hair is standing up and I am a sheet of goosebumps because my blood is running through me like a stream of melting snow.

"Why?" He says. "Do you not like it?"

"I like the color. Do you?"

"Isn't it pretty?"

At first I don't answer because I am busy. Then I don't because why, why is there a man in my dressing room — no, why is there a man in my dressing room, I ask. It gnaws at me. "Why?" he asks, "What's your name? Can I please come?" I can't answer a monosyllable and I don't know why. I come to and he is still there, looking over my shoulder as I look in the mirror, shirtless and shielded by goosebumps. I try to shove my hands through my own shirt sleeves but they are clubfists and I shove my jeans on my legs automatically, only looking at him in the mirror and clamping my mouth. Socks. Shoes. Forever. I can't answer. All I know, I can't answer. He wants me to say yes. He wants me to say no. I can't talk because a man can't fit in my dressing room. Someone outside would know that here he is. Therefore he isn't above my shoulder and I can't see with believing. Oh, oh, oh God in heaven.

No, no thanks Mom, I can't decide. I don't know what I want. The girl at the counter asks me a question and I look at her oddly. I — can't — force — nice, that's nice — out — for quite a — minute — be — cause — on — the — the — other — side, — and — above — my right — shoulder — the — man — has — asked — me — a — question — and — I — can't — no — I — won't — reply — that — would — be — giving — in. — I — know — I know — that — there — is — not — a — man — above — my — shoulder — and — to — talk — to — him would — be to — put — me on that street — bagging — groceries — and so — I — pretend

Today, SHE IS

— that — I — did not — hear her, — I — am — awkward, rude — disgraceful — socially incapable — and — I — stare — at — the — table — of — sweaters — bright Kelly pink — and rose green. — Coffee — doesn't help. — I — am — so — tired — that — I — wish — I — would — fall — into — a — volcano — down — down — down — down —down — into — depths — I don't — know of — can't imagine — where — there — will — be sleep — and maybe — I — am — incinerated — but that — would — be — okay — to sleep — in an urn, — curled — up, a pot — of sleepy — ashes. — Hello — can't I — just — say — hello — goodbye — thanks — yes — yes — yes, — okay, — no — NO — no — no — uhuh — that is all I want — uhuh — I want it — more — than — anything — I have — ever wanted — I have never — been — this hungry — before — so hungry — I — will starve — if I don't say — uhuh — affirm — that — he — is there — over — my — shoulder — Yeah, I know, — that's right Mom — no, I'm — just — tired — really tired — really, really tired, I — don't — know — why — I just — need — a nap — I think — I think — I can't say anything — because — he keeps surprising me — he is gone — but there — he — is — all — suddenly — and I want — to say uhuh — just affirm — that — he — is — there — behind — my shoulder.

I still regret the pair of shoes that I got that day and the shirt was not a good choice either, though I liked the color. Clover green.

"Seeing people who aren't really there, you mean," said my doctor at once. Damn. Yes, damn right you are. Seeing people that aren't really there. "Hallucination," suggested my dad. That is the word. Haaaal-luu-sssin-a-tion. Such a rich word to describe something that isn't even real, maybe I am just imagining the whole thing, but maybe I am hallucinating, which is a real activity.

Such an innocent word to mean Hell in your head.

PART V

"Yes, hallucinating, seeing people who aren't really there. It's possible. Might be likely." He has a goatee but at least he doesn't stroke it thoughtfully. He looks like an inquisitor, a conquistador. Tiny sad children with odd movements and disquieted fathers, weeping mothers holding wrong infants, fill the waiting room. But he is a compassionate man. I like him best of all the doctors I have had. I don't judge people by appearances. Hallucination. It rolls right off the tongue and sounds quite natural. I could do it on purpose if I wanted to. People try it all the time. People pay for this. It's so much fun it's illegal. I must not be the party type. The old Molly could have handled this with poise. That passed away. This also may.

Finally, finally, at last we sit down. I answer the librarian's question but I don't lose eye contact with him. I've been taking the medicine, but there he is at my elbow again, well what do you know. He missed me. It's been some time. Most of the time he doesn't speak.

He just begs me, implores me to speak with his eyes but I am inflexible. I am rigid. I tell him to go away and to leave me alone. He doesn't want to — just say it, he says, just say it out loud, out loud, tell me so that they can hear it. Then, then it will be real. NO. I am inflexible. You are in my head and you will stay in my head. I will not make you real with my voice. Go away, go away, go away and never come back, ever. I will not imagine you. I don't know what you look like. I won't say this again because you — are not — a — real — man. Go away; go away.

He had a beard; a plaid flannel shirt; his hair might have been reddish brownish and he seemed tall.

I close my mouth and I clamp it. Never will he hear from me one word again. He turns, he walks away and the nausea ebbs and subsides immediately and the bitterness is dissolved. I fall back in my chair, swept off my feet by sleep

Today, SHE IS

and the weight of exhaustion. Inside I was racing up the winding stair to stand at the widow's porch on the top while the bell rang and the flag blew in the wind. In exhilaration; at peace.

My mind is free. My mind is free. I run up the stairs and out of the Bastille jumping for joy and waving my arms, waving flags in the air and ringing bells. I can barely speak, I am so exhausted. I was tired before this. Now I feel that my free mind needs to sleep for years before it can be strong again.

And the cardinal hits the window.[8] Yet it pleased the Lord to put Him to grief.[9]

> *Rule wel thyself that other folk canst rede,*
> *And Trouthe shal delivere, it is no drede.*[10]

---

8. Stevens, "Casimir Pulaski Day."
9. Is. 53:10.
10. Chaucer, "Truthe."

PART VI

Did you ever know, dear, how much you took away with you when you left? You have stripped me even of my past, even of the things we never shared. I was wrong to say the stump was recovering from the pain of amputation. I was deceived because it has so many ways to hurt me that I discover them only one by one.[1]

WORDS AREN'T ENOUGH ANYWAY, even for C.S. Lewis.[2] Tread softly, for you tread upon my dreams. Yeats.[3]

What did the Psalmist think. What did the lovers, the fathers, the lonely strangers on the Titanic think as they were sinking. Could they express what they thought, finally, at that last moment?

I'm just wondering.

When I die I want to have said it all — although, come to think of it, I would have been more than happy to be dead having said nothing.

---

1. Lewis, *A Grief Observed*, 73.
2. Lewis, "The Birth of Language."
3. Yeats, "Aedh Wishes for the Cloths of of Heaven."

Today, SHE IS

I whispered hoarsely for a year. I remember going to church the first Sunday I was home, and though I was too hoarse to even reach a stage whisper, I mouthed the words of the songs. I knew then and there that I had to hoarsely sing along even though I could barely read.

I can talk now.

And now I try to write what I can't sing — to type the intonations that a word can only suggest on wings.

Can I use a cliché? The blood is stepping back into my face, a latent tide that has finally decided to roll in. Life is growing in my eyes. Blue is stepping back into my eyes on little cat feet. The flat black pupils are polishing, sparkling now and then.

My mom says that I am alive again one morning.

I feel the tinge of the sun and I can taste the rain-mellow chill like the taste of lemon tea with milk and honey in the wet summer. I drink my lemon tea with milk and Shakespeare every morning curled up on the couch. Now that I am sleeping somewhat more regularly I am trying not to live on caffeine. The taste of peace craved two, three years, a lifetime, is in my palate.

We move on into summer like we sometimes do up a green, green slope with the sky and a road of stars at the top. The sun comes out and I get a little suntan — an unnatural color on the deathly blue-white pallor of my cheeks. Warmth grows; I grow even hopeful.

Next season I do Pilates with a group of bristley older women. I study poetry and medieval art, avoid mathematics and numerals at all costs, go on afternoon walks; that spring becomes even warmer.

Oh God — I breathe, Oh God — I have survived another winter. Exhale, exhale, exhale. Inhale, inhale, inhale. I like Pilates because it takes focus. You think about breathing and you accomplish it.

PART VI

Chuck Brown is a glass man. He fixes windows, and he has a hole in his neck where the pipe went through his neck when his car ran off a cliff last November. When he gives his daughter directions he holds a microphone up to the hole and it interprets the vibrations — and his speech proceeds through a robotic voice-over that sounds like R2D2.

I think of this every time I feel a conversation brimming over with truths unsaid that drown out the small talk we thought of having. But it makes me cry to think of stroking someone's neck and saying "I love you," like a robot.

My mind lights with hope at one point because I read the story of "The Little Mermaid" again.[4] The story clicks in my heart as she rises upon the sea foam, on her tragic feet so adored, and it comes back to me how I had loved this story when I was little. I actually feel the same jittering, sparkling feeling again in a glorious flood that mangles my heart and rushes away again in a tide, leaving the remnant of a thought that floats like a little piece of kelp in my mind. I am the Little Mermaid: I gave my voice to breathe the oxygen of earth, I had to learn how to walk again.

In Heaven we'll eat words. We'll stand on them and climb them until we are up in the blue touching clouds, above the clouds, like mountain peaks — we'll walk on them, run on them, swim through them, embrace them, rip them apart and build palaces out of words.

"The" will be an entire story in itself. I'll ride "love" and "hate" and "beautiful" like stallions, bay and foaming at the mouth as they charge across bottle green fields. There is after all a "brutal materialistic air which clings only to words" as the great G.K. said waving his cane vigorously with a furious puff of his pipe.[5]

---

4. Andersen, "The Little Mermaid."
5. Chesterton, *Heretics*, 15.

Today, SHE IS

So dim below these symbols show, Bony and abstract, every one yet if true verse but lift the curse, they feel in dreams their native sun.[6]

I can imagine Paganini with the devil on his shoulder, mad because he could not speak the notes that sang in his fingers, maddened that his fiddle and bow could not contain the poem or satisfy the demon — maddened until he danced himself to an over-dose of opium. Probably. I don't know how Paganini died — I think he was ripped apart by his passions like a piece of newsprint, enflamed and engulfed by a spark.

"Hi, I'm Molly. *So* nice to meet you." I say it and I really mean it all the time to innocent little girls and innocent little boys who are my age and who think that they like me, have something in common with me, boys who maybe even get a little crush on me.

Oh, I'll crush them. What would they do if they knew that I have way more in common with a drug addict than with them? That I can read the mind of a psycho through and through while they read my lips and think that I am an open book?

This is my revenge on the cruel idiocy of immaturity. I'll let them think that. I'll spell it out plainly, lip-sync it like a bad bad singer and they will never know that I am not what they think. Self-defence.

The only difficulty is that, though the universe had been disposed of, I myself am left over. Walker Percy.[7] There is a special set of problems parasite to such advances.

It keeps occurring to me when I lose my balance in the middle of a flat surface that my left brain has been pushed out of my head through my right ear and I am having to

6. Lewis, "The Birth of Language."
7. Percy, *The Moviegoer*, 70.

PART VI

shake my head to balance it out, like a woodworker's level. It amazes me that I can hear.

Sometimes the basic fundamentals of addition required to track and carry a monosyllabic conversation are beyond me, let alone the skills to do arithmetic and cross the room without tripping, and I must be happy without them. I had always tended more to the right-brainy, English side of things anyway.

This is all so strange. These things have no place here where we are coasting. Give me my scallop-shell of quiet.[8]

Still they tear at me like sharks, conflicting to rip off the chunks of flesh and shred my heart while I curl on the floor expiring slowly from a loss of blood. I want, I want, I want — I want, I want, I want, so badly, like I have never wanted. I would push them down, stamp them out, and up around me they would flame once more, multiplied twentyfold. If I'm not dead, can't I have life? I can't function: this isn't *life*.

I am trapped in the after-math of ten days that I can't remember, held back from the enjoyment of normality by the thought process of every step I can't take and every ball I can't hit, every word I'll ever say and ever not sing, by bruises and head-aches and dizziness and the pills that keep me from the brink. I'm too exhausted for exertion, too tired to rest, I don't know sleep.

Here I am, for my family — and I am happy to be here for them. I do, I do want to be here, for them. But how *the hell* can I make it worthwhile to be there for them if I am too tired to walk upstairs half the time, and too dizzy or not mentally here the other?

No Stepford lives for me. I barely remember my own name half the time. What is this verse that people wave about me like a prophecy? To declare? How can the

---

8. Raleigh, "The Passionate Man's Pilgimage."

unspeakable be fixed by a pen?[9] How can I fix anything, declare anything — at all —

The question is a wood-pecker, sometimes shy and unobtrusive, rare and endangered, even — and then hammering, yammering, in your face, with brutal strokes of thunder. I have kept from wanting for almost a year: I've been patient. I've done what I can. Am I to have nothing? Nothing?

Make me know, God, that is all I want. With a sinking feeling in my heart I begin to feel a peace. I am knowing — and I can bite the earth. I'll just wish in one hand and spit in the other and see which fills up first.

Everyone says to follow your dreams, to do what you love. We all know, that at some point, you have to put it all behind you and move on. Maybe you're not into school. Most people aren't. But you have to be into something.

I can't be into anything. I can't do anything. I care that I can't read numbers, again and again and again, and it wrangles me like a knife digging into a wound that I can't remember algebra even though I redid Algebra 1 three times after the wreck, I can't even handle a phone number most of the time, and I have no idea what I said a moment ago. It hooks into my soul that my fingers trip up and down the keyboard, every time I sit down to play. Not only does it matter to me now, deeply — But *Hell*! My future is the only rag of the old pre–Accident Me, and it is destroying itself in the effort to be here.

My ambition is to sleep enough to function basically, to function well enough to enjoy the little things in life; not to spend my life in a pity party pushing grocery carts. Ambition for — anything — the lowest common denominator — is my last stronghold of self, a salvage rift of the old me

---

9. Lewis, "Donkey's Delight."

PART VI

that hasn't been strangled or drowned by water and boat, and that's why I am holding on to this water-pucked hand as long as I possibly can.

Just thinking of it — I have to let this go, I realize, setting my lips, I have to let this go. I can't be torn apart by caring to reach some place that I will never reach because I can barely function at all. So I cared about living? So I am motivated by goals and driven? So the old me is a bloody mangled wreck.

The little birds told me, humankind cannot bear very much reality. Burnt Norton.[10]

That is me, Paganini stripped of his instrument. Ripped apart by passions — again and again. Shrieking high in unearthly happiness, groveling in sarcastic despair, or worse, stifling by apathy. Is it always this way? Around and around again and again and again? I am Tartarus, forever and forever carrying, heaving, pushing a weight up a slope.

I find the still center again and again — only to lose it with a night of sleep. I learn my lessons — I do, again and again, and they leave me before the morning light because I don't sleep.

Humankind cannot bear much reality Burnt Norton — Burnt Everything — burnt life, blazing world, crashing down in flames to destruction, to Hell — and I see why disturbed little boys shoot everything.

Because that is the way it is. Reality is death — not just the clean death of an old man, hands folded in coffin, lily on chest, lowered into ground at a funeral, but of civilians bleeding to death internally and externally, with blood spurting everywhere while they go about their business in suits like a B movie.

---

10. Eliot, "The Four Quartets 1: Burnt Norton."

Today, SHE IS

It's true. Humankind can't bear much reality because death has no sense of proportion.

You try and you try and you try and you try, try harder, but what do you do when not even your hands will work right, let alone your mind? You solve things — but you forget, you know, and how, how on earth, are they supposed to work out in real life?

And then my stomach yawns with this pitless feeling of purposelessness. Why? It all goes back to this accident. Accident? Why do they call it an accident? Some idiot on a pleasure ride turned without bloody looking on bloody blood-thirsty stupid purpose and drove his bloody large, dangerous water-craft into me and made a bloody wreck — and now my life is a wreck, a torn, bloody, bleeding wreck of blood and feeling that we must now call "The Accident" because it is not even worth regretting because it is inevitable, irrecoverable, however incalculable. Were we to sue him out of his living daylights it wouldn't cut close to solving his debt. Money can't buy this kind of torture.

How, in heaven's name, do you know where to go when every door inside of you and out has been slammed shut, ironclad, and locked with chains in a hard-fought battle?

DAMMIT! DAMMIT! I never let myself begin to say anything else — because where will it stop? What can express it? That is the problem: words can't. I can't. I can't live. I can't function. I can't live. The monster is back and raring with fangs bared because the monster is real.

Death has no sense of proportion. It doesn't stop at the grave, at the lake, at the hospital bed — it leaps after life and eats it away while the bystanders have no idea, no idea, what is going on. The more you have to give, the more death has to devour. The more alive I am, the more I feel Death nipping away at my still-breathing corpse.

PART VI

What is worse: the pain, the eagles that eat my innards again, anew, every sunset, without fail, or the letting go, giving in and settling, calling it a day — when it's my life that I'm talking about. I can't I won't think past the peripheral. I do what is in front of me; I take the opportunity at hand; I don't think about tomorrow. I don't think about yesterday.

A pleasure is full grown only when it is remembered, says Ransom.[11] *Bonjour, tristesse.*[12] Disenchantment, disillusion; must each noble aspiration come at last to this conclusion — lassitude? Renunciation?[13] Necessity is the mother of invention.

I let go of the last plan to reach normality that I've been clinging to against everything to grasp the shards of equilibrium. It drops, and I watch it float away downstream with my goals and ambitions and lists and everything else that I had thought were good, that had made me me.

Che sera,sera. Che sera, sera. Che sera, sera.

Che sera, sera.

These little things are great to little man.[14] Che sera, sera.

I am not her, not by a long shot, not by a long time.

I come up here when I need to work things out. These things are great to little man, I realize — but what is little man to these great things?

The rock that I am lying on is right above our house. You can sun on the surface and watch the road and the hills when you are on the tier beneath the top crest, but the road can't see you.

---

11. Lewis, *Out of the Silent Planet*, 73.
12. *Bonjour Tristesse*, Dir. Otto Preminger.
13. Longfellow, "Epimetheus, Or The Poet's Afterthought."
14. Goldsmith, "The Traveler, or A Prospect of Society," 311.

Today, SHE IS

I am not gasping for death or barbarically yawping in my prayers anymore. The summer is lemon tea poured with cream and honey to cloak the arsenic—and I am dumping it in by the tablespoon — but this view here on the rock puts me into a frame of perspective.

Upside down I'm swallowed in the fishbowl of sky, a rock perch floating with the herd of clouds. I take this moment. It's mine from the sidelines. What is wrong with enjoying life from the sidelines? With hiding myself away on an island beach of perspective where I don't have to use my mind?

I can cheer from the bleachers loudly. I can easily be lost in a crowd. I'm great at making people happy. I'll cheer, I'll be lost, I'll please, I'm great at making plans. I am in the sky right here: I want to touch my plan. Please, can't this be now already?

On the rock, looking up at the sun and the sunstream through the pine tree, a memory — my own memory — comes to mind: there is me, eight years old in a Sunday dress, standing with my hands folded like a prize student, and there is Daddy sitting in a metal chair teaching us Sunday school. My sister is making embarrassing faces at a boy who is annoying her, and some little kid is raising his hand, whining "open the book, open the book!" Daddy lets it pass: Molly, what is man's chief end? he says. Man's chief end is to glorify God and to enjoy Him forever.[15] I win. I get a quarter.

The poison rushed from my veins, a tidal flood of unworded pain, brick limitations, noxious frustration, rolling out as the dam gives way and the levies topple. Man's chief end — that is my chief end. I can glorify God and enjoy Him with hair or without it, with a grocery cart or with a

15. *Westminster Shorter Catechism*, Q. 1.

sufficient I.Q, in a baseball cap. If God is with me, who can stand against me?[16]

I don't *have* to *do* anything but *be* — and enjoy it.

. . .

Driving down a hill and stopping at the traffic light I feel knives wheedling into my feet and up into my heart, which is still missing pieces in a few places: the remnants of what is so viciously shattered. *This is how it feels: so* this *is how it feels*, is what I think, nothing more. The grand passion is nothing now except another fact of life and part of myself to let go, irrevocable, in the stream of the pieces of me. The truth hits me between the eyes — I can't see because I'm dizzy. *So this is how* it *feels* — I still know, in my heart of hearts, how *this* feels.

Not that it helps to tell that to anyone with a hurting heart that I've been in that window-seat before, looking out into that vast exciting, empty world waiting to be filled, so heartless I could have blown from the top of this very high tower if I did not hold on for dear life.

No, she, he, won't believe me, how could they trust that I know all the faces of this feeling and their expressions — I know how they look when they're hungry, how they chuckle when they're independent and moan when they're not. This loss is certainty: it gives a face to the feeling. Oddly enough, this certainty is falling, finally, pushed from the tower and falling miles upon miles upon miles, always waiting for that thud that you won't be alive to hear.

I always wonder about shoppers, buzzing at the clothing racks near me in a store, if that somewhat-aged secretary ever had a lover to be the one that got away. She is Banana-Boat tanned so that her skin is the skin of a

---

16. Rom. 8:31.

Today, SHE IS

hard-bit rancher, peroxide-bleached hair (more than me), good ol' boy wrapping her waist like a hangover.

That gray boycut-headed woman has her cart where she wants it, snappy, forceful, unattractive.

The girls my own age are so intolerably much younger; centuries younger. They try on skintight violet shirts and despise the world outside their clique through uninterest. Then again, maybe the snapshot from a one-sided cell-conversation is not enough to fairly characterize a life.

Are most people happy to settle for what isn't even second or third best? Do they realize that it is *settling*?

These don't realize what the world is about, and their green-broke hearts don't know how the sight of the world wears on a broken heart as unprotected and raw as flayed skin.

They don't know, but can't the world feel that I am different — that not only am I not me, but that I am not it?

And after a while, the breathlessness is gone. Forever the moment catches you unaware, catching your breath and holding your arms so tightly that you won't fall apart, and then, some day, you look around, and you're on a plateau where the stillness fills your heart with a peace dropping slow.[17]

You take a deep breath, breathing in, still breathing, the sun is always in your eyes, and you realize that you've never been so alone, never been so alive,[18] tingling to the presence of the world around you.

Everything is illuminated in this sunset of dissolution.[19]

---

17. Yeats, "The Lake Isle of Innisfree."
18. Third Eye Blind, "Motorcycle Driveby."
19. Kundera, *The Unbearable Lightness of Being*, 4.

PART VI

Language cannot at all make manifest the quiet center we find on the other side.[20]

This was that feeling; no tears left, me walking out of a hut on a dry plateau in a breeze and watching the sun rise, a young sun, rising on blooming bushes, knowing that I am the Oldest Thing on this planet. I knew the sun when it was born. My age is unfathomable. I am an ancient of days; I survived the flood, survived the deluge and the death of the gods and the wars of men, the death of lovers and the writing of poetry, all because I did not die: I missed my death-date.

I have lived through this and I will live through everything.

The place is warmly chill; peaceful and empty. I survived feeling I realize with a rush of sunshine blowing my hair around my face. Love, hate, they mean nothing in this wisdom of years. Oh God, thank you, thank you, thank you that I survived these feelings, was all I could say in that dawn where I realized that I am still alive.

I am in Forever.

---

20. Eliot, "The Four Quartets 1: Burnt Norton."

PART VII

One thing I have desired of the Lord, that I will seek: that I may dwell in the house of the Lord all the days of my life, to behold the beauty of the Lord, and to inquire in His temple.[1]

SOMETIME BACK IN THE folds of those years I am out walking with my family, climbing a hill. My sisters run into a cave aptly called Hell's Kitchen and I follow, up the relatively flat rock surface.

The trees are shooting out at bizarre angles, hooking into my side. The sky falls like the corner of a picture, crooked, and the cirrus whirls in circles. The ground is ten feet beneath me and my knees are ten feet above my feet. The rock is sliding off the face of the earth and I have to hold on. Life becomes another bad dream and I can't reach them.

Bad depth perception is very like vertigo. First of all things you don't know where to step. The ground may be here, it may be there. It is running up an uneven slope where you have never been in the middle of a very, very

---

1. Ps. 27:4.

PART VII

dark night. There are sticks on the ground. There are holes, and there are rumps of hill. Sometimes a small animal scurries out of the way, or your dog comes underfoot. There is a cliff to one side of you and a river to the other, but you don't know which side is which. You are blind-folded. The ground shifts constantly up and down, up and down all around you like a wobbling saucer besides the fact that you have no idea where it will wobble.

That still isn't it. Would that make you lose your feet? Grow longer legs?

You have no sense of balance. None. You don't really have any sense of direction — what is up hill, down hill, right, or left. You can't trust your eyes. All that you see is murky and uncertain like you are underwater. You step very carefully, firm, precise. One foot up, one foot down; then the next. My arms hold on to the air for balance but there is nothing to hold. I proceed with caution. It's alright for a time, I guess — but I have no idea what is ahead or how I will make it there. I pick my feet up and I put them down one at a time, learning to walk.

It feels like it does to have fissured your past, to be a crazy mosaic of things that aren't you. I am walking but the ground of familiarity isn't there; I don't know where to step.

It's vertigo, someone says. I know, I know, I say flat on the ground. I would so much rather this be vertigo and in my head than that the earth is a table tilting us off the curve. So much rather.

That is where I live: on this surface of a topographical map rimmed by an infinite waterfall. I am always holding on, always barely there; just so. I don't know up, I can't tell down — I don't know what I like, I don't know what I dislike, I didn't know how Molly acts or who she is — and so I make her up like I do. Every night I spend rewriting the role. I spend every day acting out the part. Today she is

Today, SHE IS

ditzy. Today she could care less. Today she is even less dependable than you thought before. Every day she is shallow as a flat pan of water.

But still this is a world of black holes and I can't keep myself from being punctured by them, all over like child with a sheet of white paper, holed until there is not enough of me left to keep it together and I just try to cover them up, not to show, not to expose.

I see myself and I see a basket case thinly disguised by good heels holding tightly, tightly onto a crashed metabolism, violent mood swings, memory lapses, mental uncertainties, no sense of depth perception, uncertain terrain. She is an accident waiting to happen; an explosion on the verge of implosion.

Then I see myself through the mirror of my friend's eyes as we sit talking this very dark night, and that is not who I see. He doesn't see the beautiful little fool I try to be.[2] There isn't even the shadow of the fractured girl flunking ordinary life: he has no inkling of a sharred life or a shattered person.

I blamed him for looking only at the outside. He was the deep one all along. He saw through the distractions, the accents, the feints, and brought out someone that I did not know existed anymore. I knew myself only as the mirror reflected; he taught me to look through the mirror.

I don't judge others because they look dog-eared or moth-eaten. I don't hate them because they are bruised or walk into doors instead of through them. To love your neighbor as yourself implies that you love yourself. What sort of shallow pool have I been trudging for my double standards?

---

2. Fitzgerald, *The Great Gatsby*, 17.

PART VII

I think it is Lord Peter who prayed, "Lord, teach us to take our hearts and look them in the face, however difficult it may be."[3]

Immediately, I know in the core of my heart that albeit by accident I have been lying through my teeth when I believed that I was the one who was honestly aware of my self-worth.

When my friend shows me the self that he sees a brilliant light radiates through me. The eggshell of appearance splits.[4] The brokenness and the pain are still a part of me: that is because they are my past. The future is yet to be.

After the long spell of vertigo on that rock ages ago, the earth slowed to stop like a roll of film, clicking, shuddering, still. The ground balanced again. This moment is the end of my long, long spell of dispositional vertigo, of stumbling for my personality in the dark all this time. The click of relief is that the mad carousel can stop.

Everyone sees the world differently. I'm on my back on the ground, and I'm not closed up anymore. My paradigm shifts. The earth clicks into place like it did from the cliffside. The world unfolds leaf by leaf.

I used to hope that my self would flit back, a vagrant shadow like Peter Pan's. The moment it came back was more of a quake. I'm not who I was at age 15 — but healthy people change through three years. The play is over. I have myself.

The world is a maze of locked doors that open only by the turn of the screw, only by the torque of love. Death has no sense of proportion because life is beyond proportion. Life is the slashing, ripping blade, the spurting blood and

---

3. Sayers, *Gaudy Night*, 349.
4. Merrill, "Transfigured Bird."

Today, SHE IS

dripping death. It kills — and where it doesn't, there is pain, pain, pain.

Here I am, the miracle. I am Adam, I am maiden, robed and whole and solid in my place in the magical world that is itself the still center of our mad lives. The miracle happened years after the bizarre event that sparked the match. The miracle is here and now, last night and in my waking eyes this morning in the flash and fire of this lightning — rare, miraculous, flooded, revelatory.

The great and the glorious thing is that the miracle did not occur when I lived after a speedboat fell on my head. The miracle occurred years after the bystanders celebrated the survival of my shadow. The miracle occurred every day another page of my mind came back, the day that my friend introduced me to the girl who was hit by a boat.

My cage of introspection dissolves. It is a sunfall of dissolution. It still baffles me.

There is a place above our house that I love to go, a cliff on the mountainside with a rock that juts over the edge into the sky, perfect with a hollow rounded out, a prospect of perspective.

I lie here on my back, looking at the sky, and the world is a fishbowl. Look at the sky, textured with trees all around me, over me, sideways, everywhere. It sidles down to the periphery, to the extremities and dips into the hills. The sky is here, right here — we are on top of the world and you can scale the infinity by the texture of the cirrus clouds, the spindled pine stair-steps, the rush of the wind.

This pocket of the world is mine. I've seen it upside down, and that's put it inside my mind. I've been lost in it, and that's put me inside of it.

My world shifts as my heart is still. I click into place, all things are roped tight to wharf in a snug harbor. This is

PART VII

where the summer of my life begins, thinking it over in my hollow of perspective. I'm in it now, upside down, basking in the revelation of last night.

Breathless plateau, exhale, exhilaration: breathing the realization that a line has been crossed. I died, but now I live.

The world is your oyster shell, Molly, someone tells me when I turn eighteen. Here I am, 18 years old, and the world is my pearl. The world cracks open like a shell this summer, past the final barrier of high school graduation and the dreaded three-year cross-road of recovery.

I take it to heart. I always take things to heart. Life is in my heart. I can hold it and look at it in my hand, peeking through my fingers crossed over my eyes. I look at it upside down and the world opens like an oyster shell, prickling with pearls and grit.

True that euphoria waxes and wanes like feelings do. They all leave their fingerprints, their wreaths of hair, their portraits standing on the wall of the dining hall of personality.

I emerge from the cocoon of the timewarp, the mummyfolds of recovery. I don't know what will happen in the future. I don't really care. If I have lived through this, I will survive through anything and die from something. Life courses on. Rivers move into an ocean.

Now is now.

Recovery is a mountain. You walk in circles and don't feel that they are taking you anywhere. You cover the same territory again and again and again. There is too much fog to know where you are or even if you are walking uphill or downhill. But one day, you realize that you haven't reached the top yet and it is good news that you have farther to go. I can finally see that now is now.

Today, SHE IS

The sky unpeels like a Satsuma in streaks of orange sunlight. Air sparkling like champagne, leaves luscious mint-sprigs in my tea. Sunlight is juicy like an orange biting the shadows of the summer-green lawn.

The day is standing, rinsed and green. This is the day that the Lord has made: we shall rejoice and be glad in it. You know that you have never seen a morning wash a world so clean.

> November 5, 2002
>
> *Dear Molly,*
> *It has been amazing to see what God has done in your life! I'm so glad to have my friend back!*
> *Love.*
> *P.S. I left a lot of space for you to continue writing.*[5]

---

5. Anon., *Journal*, Nov. 5, 2002.

EPILOGUE

Once, driving around the lake in Mandeville, I asked Aunt Eugenie about the hurricane in New Orleans.

"It was really cathartic. You know, in all of the horrible things that happened, it was really a miracle. For the first time in years, we saw the sunlight. The woods were really overgrown: the trees were thinned out, and the next summer was the most beautiful season we had ever seen."

We are all are born into a paradigm, a world balanced like a hanging garden walled by mirrors. Then a breath of wind moves, the balance shifts, the walls shatter, the still center is lost. The paradigm shifts. Things fall apart.[1]

You fall horrifically and die.

Unless you are grounded at the center — and, then, after the earth settles, after you shake off the dust and settle your head, you slowly stand up, and see a world without walls.

Here is my coming-of-age story.

The world that I captured is the stage that I want to remember. The dark side of my mind I wished to be lost forever, unprinted negatives fade away into a forgotten dream unreal and unrealized when they see the light.

---

1. Achebe, *Things Fall Apart*.

Today, SHE IS

This is me, this is me. I am not the white grub blinking in the daylight that I see in pictures — I said. I said. I said. I said. I said. I said.

I could show you a picture of my face from that year: you will be horrified, and will think I lived in a cell. But my mind was a room with a lot of light, windows to a world of fire lit by miracles, peopled by pirates and true love, places that were not here.

I don't know the person in a photograph of myself from that period of the Recovery. I see a picture of my cat Pippin pouncing on the camera lens, and suddenly I remember her, the girl who took this shot, because I am looking through her eyes.

The prim red-haired young man looks like a bank clerk who brings Sunday flowers to the young lady of his intentions and reads the paper religiously. The person in any one of Vincent van Gogh's 69 self-portraits is really quite uninteresting. Vincent must have seen this person himself, and been so frustrated that he painted him 69 times before giving up. Only can I see the fiery kaleidoscope of his soul in a sunflower he paints; the beauty of this world was ripping his soul to shreds and the only way he could mend the tears with oil patches was to star a canvas with the night-sky.

The turning world eventually clicks into place like the spokes of a bike. Everyone has their own story of growing up. This one is mine.

Bibliography

Achebe, Chinua. *Things Fall Apart*. NY: Knopf Doubleday, 1994.
Alighieri, Dante. *The Divine Comedy*. Trans. Allen Mandelbaum. New York: Everyman's Library, 1995.
Andersen, Hans Christian. *The Little Mermaid and Other Fairy Tales*. Mineola, NY: Dover, 2003.
Anonymous. *Journal*. Personal Journal. Helena, Montana, 2002.
Augustine, Saint. *Augustine's Confessions*. Ed. Michael P. Foley. Trans. F.J. Sheed. Indianapolis, IN: Hackett Publishing Co., Inc., 2006.
Beowulf. Trans. Seamus Heaney. New York: W.W. Norton & Co., 2001.
Bonjour Tristesse, Dir. Otto Preminger. Columbia Pictures, 1958. Film.
Brabazon, James. *Dorothy Sayers: A Biography*. New York: HarperCollins, 1982.
Brock, Janelle. Interview. Moscow, ID.: September, 2010.
Chaucer, Geoffrey. "Truthe." *The Riverside Chaucer*. London: Oxford University Press, 2008.
Chesterton, G.K. *Heretics*. USA: Simon & Brown. 2012.
———. *Orthodoxy*. London: Hodder and Stoughton, 1996.
Clark, Suzanne. *Sketches of Home*. Moscow, ID: Canon Press, 1998.
Deor, "Deor's Lament." *The Oxford Anthology of English Literature: Vol. 1*. Ed. Harold Bloom et. al. Oxford University Press, Inc., 1973.
Dickinson, Emily. "I Taste a Liquor Never Brewed." *The Pocket Emily Dickinson*. Ed. Brenda Hillman. Boston: Shambhala, Inc., 1995.
Dillard, Annie. *Holy the Firm*. New York: Harper Perennial, 1998.
Eliot, George. *Middlemarch*. New York: Penguin Classics, 2003.
Eliot, T.S. "The Four Quartets." London: Faber & Faber, 1959.
Fitzgerald, F. Scott. *The Great Gatsby*, New York: Scribner, 2004.
The Fly. Dir. Kurt Neumann. 20th Century Fox, Aug. 29, 1958. Film.

Bibliography

Folds, Ben. "Still Fighting It." *Rockin' the Suburbs*. Epic Records, Sept. 11, 2001. CD.

Goldsmith, Oliver. "The Traveler, or A Prospect of Society." Harvard Classics. Vol. 41. *English Poetry II: From Collins to Fitzgerald*. New York: Bartelby.com, 2001.

Groundhog Day. Dir. Harold Ramis. Columbia Pictures. Feb. 12, 1993. Film.

The Holy Bible. New King James Version. Nashville: Thomas Nelson, 1985.

Kundera, Milan. *The Unbearable Lightness of Being*. New York: Harper & Row, 1984.

Lewis, C.S. *A Grief Observed*. New York: HarperCollins, 1989.

———. "The Birth of Language." *Poems*. Houghton Mifflin Harcourt, 2002.

———. "Donkey's Delight." *Poems*.

———. *The Four Loves*. Houghton Mifflin Harcourt, 1971.

———. *Out of the Silent Planet*. New York: HarperCollins, 2005.

The Little Mermaid. Dir. Ron Clements & John Musker. Walt Disney Pictures, Nov. 1989. Film.

Longfellow, Henry Wadsworth. "Epimetheus, Or The Poet's Afterthought." Henry Wadsworth Longfellow, 2012. Online: http://www.hwlongfellow.org.

Marvell, Andrew. "The Definition of Love." *The Poems of Andrew Marvell*. Ed. G.A. Aitken. London: Lawrence & Bullen, 1892.

Merrill, James. "Transfigured Bird." *The Kenyon Review*. Vol. 11, No. 1. Winter 1949.

Murray, Molly Miltenberger. "A Severe Mercy." Personal journal. Helena, Montana, 2002.

Newman, Randy. "Lonely at the Top." *You've Got Mail: Original Soundtrack*. Atlantic. Dec. 1, 1998. CD.

Pastan, Linda. "The Five Stages of Grief." *The Five Stages of Grief: Poems by Linda Pastan*. New York: W.W. Norton & Co., 1978.

Percy, Walker. *The Moviegoer*. New York: 1st Vintage International Edition, 1998.

Raleigh, Sir Walter. "The Passionate Man's Pilgrimage." *The Oxford Book of English Verse: 1250- 1900*. Ed. Sir Arthur Quiller-Couch. Oxford: Clarendon, 1919.

Sayers, Dorothy. *Clouds of Witnesses*. London: Hodder & Stoughton, 2003.

———. *Gaudy Night*. London: Hodder & Stoughton, 1988.

Seuss, Dr. *Horton Hears a Who!*. Random House, 1954.

Bibliography

Shakespeare. *King Lear*. The Complete Works of William Shakespeare. Hertfordshire: Wadsworth Edition Ltd., 1996.

Spellbound. Dir. Alfred Hitchcock. United Artists. Dec. 28, 1945. Film.

Stevens, Sufjan. "Casimir Pulaski Day." *Come on Feel the Illinoise*. Asthmatic Kitty. July 5, 2005. CD.

Third Eye Blind. "Motorcycle Driveby." *Third Eye Blind*. Elektra Records, April 8, 1997. CD.

Thomas, Lewis. *The Lives of a Cell: Notes of a Biology Watcher*. New York: Penguin, 1978.

"Under the Sea." *The Little Mermaid: An Original Walt Disney Records Soundtrack*. Music by Alan Menken. Lyrics by Howard Ashman. Walt Disney Records. Nov. 17, 1989. CD.

Verlaine, Paul. "Chanson d'Automne." *Poésie Française*. <poesie.webnet.fr>

Waugh, Evelyn. *Brideshead Revisited*. New York: Hachette, 2012.

Westminster Shorter Catechism. Westminster Shorter Catechism Project. 7/26/2008. Online: http://www.shortercatechism.com/resources/wsc/wsc_001.html.

Yeats, W.B. "Aedh Wishes for the Cloths of of Heaven." *The Wind Among the Reeds*. New York: J. Lane, The Bodley Head, 1899.

———. "The Lake Isle of Innisfree." *The Oxford Book of English Verse: 1250–1900*. Ed. Sir Arthur Quiller-Couch. Oxford: Clarendon, 1919.

Made in the USA
Lexington, KY
22 February 2014